TOR
and the Darknet

This book includes:

TOR: Access the Dark Net, Stay Anonymous Online and Escape NSA Spying

Bitcoin: How to Get, Send, and Receive Bitcoins Anonymously – A Darknet Guide

By Evan Lane

Contents

TOR

Access the Dark Net

Stay Anonymous Online and Escape NSA Spying

Evan Lane

Chapter 1

What is Tor?

Tor is an internet browser comprised of several networks of servers that can conceal online activities from anyone who may be watching. Tor (The Onion Router), is operated solely by volunteers dedicated to protecting the privacy of internet users all over the world. Tor uses a series of virtual tunnels making it nearly impossible for anyone to see what websites or products one may be searching online. There is no direct connection to any IP address or webpage keeping your virtual identity a complete secret. Any information one might share online via social media, blogs or anything of the like will not need to worry about invasion of privacy. Users of Tor will have access to websites they may not otherwise have access to. This is especially useful for those traveling abroad or living in countries that limit access to certain websites.

Tor helps to protect against online surveillance, which is also referred to as traffic analysis. Traffic analysis works by keeping track of the websites you visit and then advertises to you specifically. Have you ever noticed that ads to a website you visited previously will appear on the right-hand side of your email inbox or other websites you might be visiting? That is because of traffic analysis. Companies pay for traffic analysis so they can figure out who to target in the way of advertisement. Anything searched over a public network is subject to traffic analysis. The use of Tor eliminates this kind of analysis and allows users to roam freely without those pesky advertisements popping up at every turn.

There are several different destinations and sources of traffic occurring on the internet that allows others to track interests and behaviors. Not only does this make it easy for marketing companies to send ads to you based on your searches, but it also makes it easier for hackers to access your searches. This is a criminal activity in which they look into your social media accounts to see if you are on vacation so they can rob the home. Hackers can also literally wreak havoc by destroying credit scores and discovering an exact location. While the Dark Net sounds daunting, it is really a great place for people to browse the internet and post freely without having to fear being monitored.

Use of a public internet like Internet Explorer, Firefox or Google Chrome makes it easy for data to be collected in what are known as packets. Internet analysis occurs when the packets are broken down. From there comes the payload, which is the data that was collected as well as the header that directs traffic online. Payload information is what is embedded in emails, audio files or standard webpages. The payload is usually encrypted, but the traffic analysis tends to expose the majority of the information of what is being explored on the internet. The header is what traffic analysis focuses on because it will show the source, time, ultimate destination (webpage you ended up on) and the size of files discovered on the internet.

Downloading Tor is a very simple process. There is no program to purchase nor is there any lengthy instructions to follow. If one wishes to use the Dark Net, all they need to do is download the Tor browser. This can be done easily by visiting www.torproject.org/download.download. Once you've arrived at the webpage, it will provide all sorts of useful information on how to properly use the Dark Net and any system requirements necessary for proper use of the browser. Once the Tor browser has been downloaded, simply do what you have always done on the internet except now you can do so worry free!

Tor can be used the minute the download is complete. Tor is one of the most secure browsers in the world, and it is good to know that there are government agencies all over the world who keep an eye on Tor. The Federal Bureau of Investigation is included. As a matter of fact, the FBI admittedly attempted a malware attack on Tor, which was unsuccessful.

Naturally, as with anything, there are also weaknesses with the Tor browser. However, to this day, it has not been penetrated or taken down by any malicious attack. When used properly, any activity online will be hidden by the hidden networks utilized with the Tor browser.

Computers using Tor are less likely to be attacked or compromised. There are other steps one can take to keep your online activities completely hidden.

First, Tor recommends *not* using Windows, which includes the use of Tor bundles. Specifically, the Tor bundles have weaknesses that were targeted by the FBI a few years ago, in their attempted attack on the Tor networks. Workstations should not be created while using Linux in conjunction with Tor. There needs to be a proxy (the best is Privoxy) used in addition to browsers with a firewall for any data that might be visible outside of the browser's protection. One can use Clearnet, but if that fails, Whonix or Tails are great to keep all data from being leaked. You will always want to have a firewall to ensure third parties are unable to access data to perform the traffic analysis we discussed previously.

If you are using external (or even internal) storage, you will want to ensure encryption. Currently, the LUKS program is great for this and is one of the options that will pop up while you are installing the Tor browser.

When using Tor, always make sure that your computer is up to date. Any time you are prompted to run updates, do so to keep Tor working properly and to make sure your version of Tor is always up to date. This allows the user to avoid new security breaches as well as using their workstations. If it seems like it has been a while since the last update, you can always double check the Tor site to see if there have been any new software updates that need to be downloaded. You will not want to miss any of those so the computer and internet browsers will always be properly protected.

While a lot of programs you might use require Java or Flash, you are going to want to disable those. While using Tor, you might come across a website that says those programs are required. The use of either of those allows for traffic analysis. Most of the things you see with Java or Flash are not anything important. It tends to be a Gif or something along those lines that can easily be ignored and are not required for you to access a website fully. If, for some reason, you absolutely do need to enable scripting, do so temporarily and make sure you disable it again before leaving the site.

Rid your computer of cookies or data that a website may send to the advertisers. This is a manual step required as there is no way for the Dark Net to complete it for you. You will see an add-on called *self-destructing cookies* that will automatically destroy all cookies on your computer.

It is also a good idea to use a laptop as your main workstation because it is mobile. Additionally, laptops are a little easier to discard in the instance that becomes a necessity. Finally, avoid using Google when possible. It is one of the most commonly used search engines all over the world meaning it is the most heavily watched in the way of traffic analysis.

While using Tor, the environment used along with it is also important. A little later, we are going to talk about some of the weaknesses of Tor, which is why the environment is important. There are some things you can do to make sure that hackers or traffic analysis don't occur.

1. As mentioned, a laptop is the best type of computer to use because it is mobile. It is best to use Tor anywhere except home. Specifically, this is when you are searching information that could be considered sensitive. Public networks are easier to monitor, but by using Tor and the fact that there are several thousand people using public networks in your area, you will be much safer online. Hackers are usually able to connect to your computer without your knowing, which is another reason the Tor network is so great. If you do not use Tor at home, you will not be tied to a location, making it more difficult for hackers to find any personal information about you. If advanced threats are a fear of yours, take your laptop to

a coffee shop for any internet browsing you may wish to do. However, Tor networks are near impenetrable so using them at home is safe so long as you are not worried about what kind of information you are searching online or what kind of things you are posting on any social media accounts you may have.

2. Online activities in which you do not wish to be tracked and you have chosen to leave the house, remember to leave your cell phone at home. If, for some reason, you believe your online activities are being tracked, your cell phone (turned on) at home will lead others to believe you are at home and they will attempt to look into the IP address associated with your house. If you leave your phone at home, it is a good idea to make sure people know what time you are expected to return so there are no concerns if they attempt to call several times and are unable to reach you. Likewise, there are messaging applications you can use over Tor that are not traceable and you should be able to communicate with people through those messaging apps.

3. It is always wise to monitor how much time you are spending in one location while using Tor. There are some hackers (or government agencies) who look for people that are using public networks. It is recommended to avoid using the same public location on a regular basis.

Try to set up several places like Starbucks, McDonalds and any other place that offers free Wi-Fi so there is no way to tie you to any one location. The best protocol is to use a location once and then never go back. That is incredibly difficult for people who have no car or live in a small town with fewer choices as far as free Wi-Fi is concerned. Continuing to use the same location makes it easier for the people who work there and those who frequent the location to remember what you look like, the kind of car you drive and so on. Always keep in mind that people who work in those places tend to start to recognize regulars and it is best if you can mix up locations and not go back at all, or at the very most every few weeks.

With those recommendations, out of the way, we are going to talk a little about the fear of using the Dark Net. The name itself sounds daunting, almost illegal, right? There is not anything to worry about. It is actually very safe and legal. Making sure you have a positive outlook when it comes to Tor is going to be crucial. It will also make you feel more at ease while using Tor. Below are some more steps on how to use Tor and feel safe while doing so.

1. It is a good idea to create an online persona or virtual identity while using Tor. Use something that will not be tied to you in any way. For instance, do not use any moniker you have used anywhere in the past and avoid

using any variation of your name or personal email address. Likewise, you are going to want to create a new email address that you use specifically for Tor. Again, make sure you do not use your name or any part of it while creating an email address you use on Tor. Ultimately, you are separating your personal life from your Tor life. It is kind of cool when you think about it that way.

2. Make all new accounts with your new virtual identity and be very careful not to get your virtual accounts and personal accounts mixed up.

3. Try not to use your virtual accounts on Clearnet unless there is no other option.

4. Earlier we talked about leaving your personal cell phone at home if you are going to use a public network to access Tor. Along those lines, it is wise to have a disposable phone for any phone calls or text messages you may want to send while using the Tor network. Believe it or not, your cell phone can be tracked easily. If you choose to use a disposable phone, make sure your personal phone is turned off while using Tor for an added safeguard. When purchasing a disposable phone, use cash and not a debit or credit card. Also, remember to never use a SIM card on the phone nor should you activate it near your home address. This should be used in conjunction with your

virtual identity and kept separate from anything to do with your personal life. That point cannot be driven home enough. The phone and Dark Net identity should absolutely be kept separate.

Tor is great for keeping online activities secret because of the increased privacy and security associated with using the Dark Net. This is great for keeping hackers or government agencies from looking into your online activities. Sometimes, you're using a virtual identity may raise some red flags, which is another reason you want to keep personal life matters separate. This includes family members.

Chapter 2

Browsing the Internet Anonymously with a VPN

Internet privacy is a concern for everyone this day and age. Most people would like to know just how secure their activities online are and how much of the things they browse are traced back to their IP address. To be perfectly honest, as we previously touched on, everything done online can be traced back to the user. Whether one uses public or private Wi-Fi, anything that is searched online can be traced to the device you use and therefore linked to you directly. While most people are not engaging in any illegal activities, it is quite disturbing to know that anyone can look at what we are doing online at any given moment. There are millions and millions of other people using the internet who choose not to take special precautions. Without taking the extra step to protect your online activities, anyone from the NSA, FBI, and general hackers can see what you search while on the internet.

One of the questions you might be asking right about now is, how can internet activity be traced to you personally? The answer to that is quite simple. It is the IP address that is tied to your device. The IP is a code uniquely associated with your devices that are network enabled. It gives internet servers a general location of where you are geographically. Each time you are accessing an online service or website, the IP address must pass through those servers, making your activity visible to those hackers and marketers we discussed earlier.

Any information that passes through these servers simply lets them know which language should be displayed on the website, what content the user is going to have access to and whatever advertisements they deem relevant to your specific search. Overseas, content can be limited and therefore limit your access to information based on the location the IP provides. Also, there are websites that draw attention from law enforcement agencies worldwide. Specifically, websites such as those related to pornography or BitTorrent.

There are some ways to hide your online activities and, in this chapter, we are going to specifically address the use of a VPN along with Tor.

A VPN is an abbreviation for Virtual Private Network. This allows a connection to any internet service through your personal server by a provider of the VPN. Information going from your tablet, phone, or computer through the BPN server is encrypted. By using the BPN. You are provided additional privacy by hiding your internet activities from the Internet Service Provider (ISP) and anyone else who may be looking in on your activity. Using a VPN in addition to the Tor network allows users to avoid censorship while at work, school, the government, and even the internet service provider. The use of a VPN creates what is known as a *geospoof* of your actual location meaning you can have access to many services that might have previously been denied. This usually happens if you are traveling outside of the United States or perhaps if you are in a geographical location that prohibits access to certain websites. The added security of a VPN can also keep you protected against hackers if you are using a public Wi-Fi network. It also lets the user download anything safely.

Anyone can get a subscription to a VPN and we are going to go over exactly how they work. The user will sign up for a service plan with a company of their choice. There are quite a few VPN services and later in this chapter, we will talk about some choices you have in regards to selecting the one that will be right for you. Once the user is on a service plan, they will be able to download software and any applications necessary to run the software on their device or devices. From there, the user can select a location for their server and quite easily connect. The VPN hides the IP address and you will be assigned on specifically associated with the server chosen when you signed up for the service. Internet activity is encrypted and entirely hidden from everyone so you are free to use the network you have set up as well as any public networks without having to worry that the pages you are searching can be traced back to you.

When you are considering selecting a VPN, it is important to search for specific features surrounding connectivity and security. The first step is finding a VPN that has the bandwidth you desire. Bandwidth functions by data transfer limits, which are usually imposed by the ISP in addition to the VPN you have selected. Most VPNs have unlimited bandwidth. While looking for the VPN that is right for you, just double check to make sure there are no bandwidth limits as those tend to slow down internet browsing.

Next, select a VPN with several different connections. Because most people use many different devices from smartphones to laptops and tablets, you are going to want to choose a VPN that allows you to connect all your devices.

Lastly, you are going to check the strength of the encryption of the VPN. When it comes to this service, there are two different strengths. They are 128 or 256 bit. 256 is going to be the best, so you will want to try to find a VPN with 256 bits. Additionally, you are going to want to find a VPN that allows you to choose your security settings. It is important to note that encryption tends to slow down network connections which means the strength of the encryption is going to help optimize connectivity in relation to security and speed. Of course, this all is dependent on what you plan to use the internet for as well.

You are also going to want to look for the size of the VPN network. It is important to locate a VPN with a minimum of fifty servers in the entire network. With more servers, available to use, you are going to have more access to bandwidth. Also, you will want to see what the system requirements and compatibility are. This is a simple step. All that needs to be done here is to ensure that the VPN is going to be compatible with every device you wish to connect it to. Most VPNs can be used with Mac or Windows operating systems. Ideally, you are going to want to find one that will also work with all your mobile devices, tablets included.

Finding a VPN that is easy to use is also crucial, especially when you are just starting to explore Tor and using the VPN as an added security measure. The easiest VPNs to use are those with automatic setups and those who have great customer service ratings just in case you need assistance. Below you are going to see a list of the top three rated VPNs among Dark Net users that are going to help you add protection to your internet searches.

HideMyAss – The name itself is quite funny, but we are going to talk about its attributes. This VPN comes with unlimited bandwidth, can be used on PC or Mac and with Linux or iOS. It is also able to be used on Android products. This service allows for two connections on each account, has 256-bit encryption, a worldwide network, live phone, chat, or email support available 24/7, and a thirty-day money back guarantee. The cons to this service are that it is known to be unreliable and sometimes slower than it should be. While it boasts 24/7 live support, their responses to email can be slow. Another con is that the software itself is a little more complicated than it should be, so beginners might want to shy away from this one.

Express VPN – This service gets a 9.5/10 rating among users. It offers the fastest connections and the strongest encryption available. Naturally, there are pros and cons with any service, and we will cover both, just as we did previously. Express VPN has more pros than cons, which is a great start. With this service, you will receive unlimited bandwidth, automatic setup, two connections with each account purchased, a worldwide network, compatibility with Android, iOS, Mac, Linux, and Windows. The connection is extremely reliable and very fast. It comes with the highest encryption at 256 bits and has options that are entirely customizable to your needs. They also offer 24/7 live chat support, a referral program, fast email responses and a money back guarantee. It seems that there is just one con with this service and it is that they do not offer any phone support. It is still highly rated and a favorite among users.

IPVanish – Overall, users of the VPN rate it 7/10, which is not a bad score. The connection is fast; you are allowed two connections per account, is compatible with Windows, Linux, Android, and Mac and has a worldwide network. The bandwidth matches the others with a 256-bit encryption. They offer a one week money back guarantee. IPVanish also provides a reliable, fast connection as well as an automatic setup. This VPN is not compatible with iOS, and while they say they have 24/7 email support, their responses tend to be slow. There is no phone support nor do they provide live chat options for assistance. In general, IPVanish does provide good connectivity, reliability, and speed. However, if you are using iOS, you are going to want to use either Express VPN or HideMyAss to get the coverage you need while using Tor.

There are many ways in which to conceal your online activities from those who have prying eyes. VPNs are one of the best ways to add an extra layer of protection to using the Tor network. Above are the highest rated VPNs.

Chapter 3

Using Tor for Online Anonymity

By now, you should have downloaded Tor, and this comment will address how to use Tor without VPNs or any other add-ons. Tor is easy to use. In this chapter, we will talk about how to use Tor and the differences you might see in the browser you just downloaded as opposed to what you are used to using. Tor is simple, but also incredibly different than what you are used to, and it is important you understand how to use it to avoid your information being compromised while surfing the web.

Once you have installed the browser on your computer or device, you will see a folder entitled *Tor Browser*. In there, you will find a link that is entitled *Start Tor Browser.exe*. Click on that link, and it will open a brand-new web browser. Next, you will be asked if you are sure you want to connect to the Tor network or if you would first prefer to configure your network settings. It is easiest if you choose to simply connect. There will be a few moments before the browser fully connects to the network. Once there, you will be able to surf the web anonymously.

If you want to be sure that you are correctly connected to the Tor network, you can connect to www.whatismyip.com. This is going to allow you to see where your IP address appears on a world map. If you are correctly connected to the Tor network, you should see your IP somewhere away from your home address. If you this, you are connected to Tor and ready to start securely browsing the internet.

Tor specifically is used to browse the internet safely and securely. However, it is important to keep in mind that you still have programs on your computer not protected by Tor. That means they are not secure and using them will make your information visible for anyone to see. Once you have the Tor browser installed, it is best to do everything through that browser. As we previously touched on, you will want to make sure you have a new virtual identity to avoid crossing the personal lines with those you wish to remain anonymous.

To explain how Tor works a little further, we are going to touch on site connections. The encryption process for this goes through the SSL or TSL. If encrypted sites are not being utilized, there is a risk of exposure to anyone who might be looking for this kind of mistake. There are always going to be people on Tor who are looking to exploit first time users. Before you get to looking through sites, make sure you have that anonymity. As we discussed in the VPN chapter, you can also add an extra browser powered by the Electronic Frontier Foundation that makes sure any sites used are going through the very secure SSL or TSL lines.

Always be careful of what kinds of sites you visit. Using Tor does not necessarily mean no one can see what you are doing, especially if you make one of the crucial mistakes we have previously discussed. Viruses and malware can still be installed on the computer if you do not pay attention to the kinds of sites you are accessing. Tor is meant to secure the sites you visit, not keep malicious attacks from happening. Making sure that your malware software is up to date is an important part of using Tor responsibly.

Most of us do not want others to know what we are researching online. It has nothing to do with the type of content we search and more to do with just wanting privacy, and there is nothing wrong with that. We all want to know that we are surfing the web anonymously. Without using Tor, anything you look at on the internet can be traced back to you. As we discussed previously, any ads related to sites you may have visited in the past are geared specifically toward you and are a result of the traffic analysis reports provided to marketing agencies. While we are doing nothing illegal, it is hard to imagine people being able to use information from websites we visit and create ads on our home screens or emails based on the sites we visited. Realistically speaking, we do not just have to worry about marketing either. Hackers, NSA, or FBI agents can easily see what we are doing online. As law-abiding citizens, we only need to worry about hackers who intend to do harm by stealing our personal information, which can be easily seen over the internet. Every day, hackers work hard to crack passwords for emails and bank accounts to take what we work so hard for.

The IP address you use in conjunction with your Wi-Fi is what tracks your online activity and is unique to you and the devices you use. The IP is associated with your computer and any devices used on that network. The provider is given your geographical location of whatever device is being used on the network. Every time you visit a website, the IP address pings on numerous servers which not only tells traffic analysis agents what kind of content you are searching but also where you are searching from.

In general, information sent over the servers lets the website know what kind of content to display. This includes the language it should be in, which is determined by where you are in the world. It also decides what kind of advertisements to show on the page, which is based on the types of websites you visit on a regular basis. Obviously, there will be websites you will want to refrain from visiting even while using Tor. Those include anything of a pornographic nature and those that government agencies might be watching. Anything related to treason or uprisings should always be avoided. There are also some keywords that when typed in a search engine (remember, we talked about avoiding using Google) that government agencies are specifically looking for. Even typing those into Tor could attract unwanted attention.

We touched earlier on the *geospoof*. This allows you to access services you may have been denied before based on your location. There are some countries that do not allow access to simple sites like MSN or Google, which is where Tor will come in handy. These along with VPNs can protect you from hackers while using public networks.

Chapter 4

How to use Tor Without Getting Caught

As we previously discussed, Tor is a volunteer operated network of people who provide people with secure and private ways to browse the web. Using Tor is done through a series of virtual tunnels and never makes a direct connection, which is what makes it hard for information on the Tor network to be traced. The use of indirect connections allows users to feel free to share any information they please through public networks and do not have to concern themselves with compromising their privacy. This also allows the user to access certain areas on the internet that are blocked otherwise.

Tor helps keep people safe from the most common ways others can see online activities, which is in the form of the aforementioned traffic analysis. Once Tor is downloaded (which at this point it should be) you will be able to avoid surveillance agencies and keep your internet activities concealed. Earlier, we talked about using Tor safely, and this chapter is going to go into a little more depth.

1. The most important rule is never to use Windows. Additionally, you will want to avoid using the Tor

Browser bundle in conjunction with any Windows based program. The FBI exposed some of the vulnerabilities of Tor in their attempted takedown of Freedom Hosting. The Tor Browser Bundle has several vulnerabilities that are only exposed while using Windows based programs. Again, avoid Windows with Tor.

2. Download Linux. If you cannot create your workstation with Linux, there are other options available. Linux, in general, works best with Tor and can keep up with the updates Tor has on a regular basis. It also works well with Privoxy and any firewalled web browsers on Clearnet. However, you can also try Whonix or Tails if Linux just is not compatible with your workstation. These applications take the guesswork and questions out of your searches and do all the work on your behalf. All outgoing access is firewalled, so third parties are unable to leak your data concerning what you are searching on the internet as well as your geographical location.

3. Make absolutely sure that all your storage is encrypted. LUKS is a great and very safe addition, and every Linux variation offers automated setup of this program during its installation process.

4. Always remember to keep your computer up to date. We touched on updating in a previous chapter, and it is incredibly important always to perform updates when

prompted. If you are using Tails or you have built a workstation on your own, you are going to want to update just to keep your vulnerabilities at the lowest risk levels. You can perform an update each time a new session is initiated, but at the very least you will want to update daily. Tails is great in that it will prompt you to update when the program starts if a vital update is necessary.

5. Disable Flash, JavaScript, and Java. Another one we touched on briefly before. If you come across a site that requires any of these, go to another site. There are plenty out there that do not require any of those programs to function properly. Those programs are used for traffic analysis, and you will want to avoid them, enabling them only as an absolute last resort. If you do enable any of those programs, make sure to disable it before leaving the site.

6. Always delete cookies and any local data being sent to you by a website. Tails nor Tor can do this on their own and require some manual adjustments made by the user. You are also able to add on something known as *self-destructing cookies* which will take care of cookies on your behalf just in case you forget.

7. Never use Google as your primary search engine. This cannot be reiterated enough. You can use an engine known as *startpage* as that is the default search engine

used on the Tor network, meaning it will be easy to access once you have the Tor browser. This search engine never requires the use of CAPTCHAs which is a great bonus.

8. Your workstation should always be a laptop. Being portable is important, and they are easy to destroy or dispose of in a pinch.

Another way to make sure your information is totally secure is to have a clean environment for your system to run. When we say clean, we do not mean dust free or clutter free. It is an environment in which you are not accessing regularly. These steps will ensure you are never at the same location, making it even harder to track your online searches.

1. Limit the amount of time you spend on Tor at any given location. Attacks of the correlation persuasion take a bit of time although they can be done in less than twenty-four hours. There are things known as Jackboots that rarely appear on the day you use Tor at a public location, but it is possible for them to be there the very next day. That is a great reason to avoid using Tor in the same place on a regular basis.

2. Avoid using Tor anywhere near your home. This is especially important if you are working on sensitive information. Even offline, computers tend to remain

connected and often they can connect automatically. To truly keep prying eyes away from your system, do not use Tor longer than a full day (24 hours) at any one location. Once you have used Tor at any given location, it is best to consider it trashed and move on. This works well even if Jackboots appear four to six months afterward. Again, it is always easier for people to remember the face of someone who comes in regularly over those they may have only seen once. If you do not have the convenience of living in a big city, consider traveling further out. It is difficult in smaller and sparsely populated towns, but it is doable if you want to protect your online identity.

3. Do not forget to leave your cell phone at home, turned on if you are going to be using Tor and do not want people to be able to track you.

This might sound weird, but it is good to have the correct mindset as it pertains to anonymity while using Tor and the Dark Net. Most users get caught for making an easy mistake like accidentally using their personal email address as opposed to the virtual reality email. You need to train yourself to have mental discipline when it comes to using Tor, and you will have nothing to worry about. Below are some ways you can work on training your mind.

1. If you plan on using any public Wi-Fi, you are going to have to make new accounts that match the pseudonym

you created. If you have not created your virtual identity (pseudonym) yet, you are going to want to do that immediately. It is crucial to online safety and security. Never mix your online persona with your personal accounts. A good example is on Facebook. Make sure you never connect your real-life email address with the pseudonym for Instagram on the computer you use Tor. It will be much safer to wait until you get home.

2. On occasion, you will have to answer the phone. As we previously mentioned, it is wise to have a prepaid phone. In some countries, it is a little more difficult than others, but always remember that where there is a will, there will be a way. Always pay in cash to both purchase the phone and purchase minutes. Never turn on the prepaid phone in a ten-mile radius of your home. Never use the phone if the battery cannot be removed. Do not insert a SIM card from any other device and never give out the number or admit to having a prepaid phone to anyone who is unaware of your pseudonym. It is hard to keep secrets from family members, but this does include them if they are unaware of your virtual identity.

3. Never do anything related to your pseudonym on Clearnet unless it is a last resort. For example, if you use a program that specifically prohibits the use of Tor (there aren't many, but they are out there). If you have to use

this service, take added steps to ensure your location is not visible to anyone.

Hidden services have been hotly debated and have made an appearance in the news lately. Recently, there was a takedown of two high-profile hidden services. Silk Road and Freedom Hosting were the sites involved. This turns out to be a bad/good news scenario. The bad news is that it shows the weaknesses in these hidden services. The good news is that the NSA does not seem all that interested in them.

Hidden services tend to be run under the control of another person meaning they can be compromised or vulnerable by another party. It is always important to make sure the anonymity of that service is protected because if it is compromised just one time, there is no going back.

The gist of this chapter is that it is difficult to have an online persona and a real-life persona. There is no technology in the world that can do this on its own. To be truly anonymous means you need to be able to take actions from the real world and mitigate weaknesses in the virtual world, pay attention to the little details and have a clear mind. There are some hackers who just happen upon information by sheer luck while others spend their entire day trying to bring down a network for no good reason. If a user makes a mistake that could have been avoided, it could have devastating consequences. While all of this may sound daunting, I implore you not to give up. Internet security is something we should all take an interest in and not simply because traffic analysis is performed and we are getting ads. There are malicious people out there looking to make another life hell. Keep working with Tor, and you will never look back.

Chapter 5

Using Bitcoins to Remain Anonymous

While remaining anonymous on the internet, you might have to use money to make purchases. It is incredibly difficult to manage funds or make purchases online while using a pseudonym. Thankfully, there is a remedy to that problem, and it is called Bitcoin. If used correctly, this service can keep your personal information safe and makes it next to impossible for anyone to be able to compare the online persona to that of the real-life person. Below, we are going to provide you with a step by step guide to setting up a Bitcoin account and how to use it. This will provide details on the Bitcoin environment, how you can communicate with others, browse the web anonymously and how to send or get Bitcoins.

1. The first step is to download Tails. It is on the Linux operating system that can be used with a DVD or USB stick. You will not have to install this on a computer, which takes the anonymous level up a notch. Tails comes with all the software pre-installed on the disc or a USB drive. Once it is ready, it is going to route all traffic through the Tor network that you have already created. The best way to get Tails is from someone who already

has a copy. They can transfer it onto a USB and hand it right over. You can also download it from their official Tails website. While it is not incredibly difficult, you will need to install it manually. Instructions are provided, and they are well written as well as easy to follow.

2. Fire Tails up. If you downloaded from the website, click on the link. Otherwise, you will insert the DVD or the USB to start Tails. Newer computers automatically detect the insertion of a new device and will ask to start up. There are occasions in which you will need to go through the BIOS startup. If you have already set up your online persona (you certainly should have by now) you are going to want to use that when accessing Tails. Never use personal information. This includes browsing, chatting with other users, typing a document and Bitcoin transactions. Always keep your browsing focused and never log in to any personal media account while you are on Tails.

3. In this step, you are going to enable something called *persistence*. This step is required because without it you will be unable to save anything in Tails. There is a heading entitled Applications. From there you will select Tails and then choose the option to configure the persistent volume. For this option to work, the USB drive will be necessary to create the Tails Installer program. If

you made the stick manually, it will be necessary to copy Tails with a different USB drive. The Tails installer process is found in Applications > Tails > Tails Installer. From there, you will be required to create a passphrase. As with any passphrase, the longer it is the better because it will be more difficult to crack. Every time you use tails, you will be required to enter the passphrase so make sure it is something that is both lengthy and difficult for others, but easy for you to remember. During this process, Tails will ask you what information you want to store. Keep in mind that the less information stored within Tails, the more secure your connection will remain. Unfortunately, this also means you are going to have to remember which items you use in Tails and set them up each time you login to the service. The recommendation is that you use Bitcoin, Personal Data, GnuPG, Icedove, Network Connections, Pidgin, or Browser Bookmarks. Once you are done there, restart Tails with persistence enabled. Once again you must enter the passphrase. Anything done in the persistence folder can be saved when the computer is shut down.

4. Set up a KeePassX. This is a lifesaver for those of us using the Dark Net. It stores all your passwords meaning you will only be required to remember a couple. KeePassX is found under applications > accessories > KeePassX. You will need to create a password in this database by

following the path: File > Create New Database. There is a program called Diceware that you can select a very long yet easily remembered password allowing access to KeePassX. This password will be the second of three passwords you will be required to remember. All passwords created from them on out will be remembered via KeePassX. This will be saved to the persistent folder. When creating a new password, you will click on the key (it should be yellow) and will say add new entry. Give it a title and enter in the required information. The button you should pay attention to is called Gen, which is on the right side of the Repeat field. Select Gen by clicking the button and it will generate a password on your behalf. You can determine the length of the password and if you want it to have special numbers or characters. To keep things at the highest level of secure, it is best if you do not even look at the password. There is no need to see it or know it since it will be saved for you. If by some chance someone is looking at your screen, all that can be seen is stars and not the password itself. Generating the password is automated. Once it is done, copy and paste it into the site you need to access.

5. The next step is to get a PGP Key. In Tails, you will have to make a new PGP Key which can be found by clicking Applications then Utilities followed by Passwords and Keys. Next, you are going to click the symbol that looks

like a blue plus sign. That can be found under the GnuPG key. From there, enter your name and email address. Make sure it is the pseudonym you created, especially if you intend on sending encrypted emails. The password here will be required each time you need to decrypt a file, or an encrypted email is sent to you.

6. From there you will set up Electrum. In your Bitcoin Wallet, you can click on applications > Internet > Bitcoin Wallet. Electrum is thought of as a lightweight wallet according to Bitcoin standards. You will not need a copy of Blockchain, and it relies instead on other types of nodes. Several nodes, in fact. If you wish to see your balance, you can enter the bitcoin address into your Blockexporlorer. This is done by using Blockcypher so you can see your balance and any transactions that occurred with the Bitcoin account. It is in this area you will create your wallet. There is no need for anything other than the standard wallet, which works perfectly fine. In there you will see thirteen words typed in English that are representative of the wallet seed. Anyone with that seed combination can access your wallet and steal Bitcoins from it. It is important you are very careful with where you store those thirteen words. With KeePassX already installed, it will be easy to store the words in that program securely. You can also write them down and lock the combination of words away if you find it difficult

to paste it in the comment field. Press the proceed button and you will be able to put the wallet seed in the window that pops up. After that, choose your password. Again, we recommend you create one with KeePassX. This password will be required for every transaction. With that setup, you will be able to send and get Bitcoin payments. Addresses and balances as they relate to the Bitcoin can be found under the addresses heading. What is great here is you can also create more than one wallet under the same identity. You are also able to create a new wallet just for a single transaction. Keeping your wallets separate makes it much simpler to keep money separated for accounting purposes or for your privacy in general.

7. Next you will want to use the XMPP and OTR to communicate. Pidgin is the program used when chatting with other users. It is difficult to get an anonymous email account, so some find it easier to chat with people by using the Pidgin tool. There is one issue with this in that you cannot get messages when you are not online. You can install Pidgin by going to Applications > Internet > Pidgin. After that, you are going to be able to access Pidgin, add your account and then check XMPP as your protocol. Many of the XMPP servers are public. To provide an accurate example, we selected the search engine entitled duckduckgo for its privacy friendly standards. Once there, you can choose your user name

and enter duckgo.com for the domain. Next, you will choose a password and select the box entitled *create new account on the server*. Close the window and reconnect so the new chat account with Pidgin is enabled. When the window is reopened, it might ask you to reenter your user name and password. Once again, we will mention KeePassX for this. It is much easier to store them there rather than having so many to remember. To use the secure chat function, select the OTR encryption option. You will do that by clicking OTR > Start Private Conversation. You can also choose to verify the integrity by clicking OTR > Authenticate Buddy.

8. In this step, you are going to make sure that you back everything up by using PGP. Of all the steps, this is the trickiest because it takes some effort. The more of your effort put into locking the key means that it will be less accessible should you need it. We recommend a very strong password by using Diceware when you create the PGP Key. The key can be loaded onto any USB device and left with friends or a family member, or a lawyer or safe deposit box if necessary. We also recommend that a regular backup of all documents you do not want to lose is done. This also applies to KeePassX and your Bitcoin wallet. Select all files and the folders you want to backup. From there, right-click the selection and click encrypt. You may see a popup window asking which keys you

would like to encrypt. From there, you will only need to select the PGP key. It is important to avoid clicking the sign option. When it comes time to decrypt a file, all you will need to do is double click the file labeled .gpg then enter the password for the PGP key.

9. The last step in this process is to repeat all steps one through eight for each identity created. There will need to be different USB drives with Tails for every pseudonym you create. Each stick should have a different password, separate KeePassX databases, and different PGP keys.

Now that we have those steps completed, we can briefly touch on how to get Bitcoins. In this case, you should remember and be aware that no matter how you acquire the Bitcoins, the actual transaction is difficult to keep entirely anonymous. For your convenience, we have detailed a few of those options below that show a more private way to make Bitcoin transactions.

Bitcoins can be purchased in person through what are known as bitcoin meetups which are found under the marketplace option under the Mycelium wallet. This is only something that can be done on the Android version. You are also able to find traders with local Bitcoin platforms.

You can also get Bitcoins from an ATM. There are many of these in countries all over the world, and alternatively, there are countries in which Bitcoin ATMs are incredibly rare. You can find the Coin ATM Radal to locate Bitcoin ATMs in your area. You will need to click on the *other services* option on the left-hand corner, or you could miss places that offer to sell Bitcoins as vouchers.

If you choose to spend bitcoins, you should also accept them as a form of payment. In doing this, acquiring them will be an unnecessary step. Bitcoins received are not anonymous because somewhere there is a record that they were paid to you. It is a bit of a double-edged sword. If you are looking for convenience and it does not matter if there is a record, accept bitcoins as a form of payment. If anonymity is more important, finding Bitcoin ATMs is the way to go.

The last thing we will talk about in this chapter is mining bitcoins. This is not the most profitable way to get them but is a fine alternative. To mine Bitcoins, you will need a mining machine paid for with cash. You will have to plug it in, point it toward the mining pool, and watch the earnings come to you.

Chapter 6

Web Levels and Pseudonyms

Because we have mentioned it a couple of times, and because it is important, we are going to touch briefly on the use of Dark Net personas. The Dark net is the internet that is hidden beneath the actual internet and purposely kept from the view of people who are considered *ordinary* web users. One of the most normal misconceptions is that the Dark Net is hard to access, which as you should know by now is untrue. Using the Dark Net requires no special skill or knowledge, you simply have to download the TOR browser, and you are good to go.

Before we get into pseudonyms, we will cover what the differences are between deep web, dark web, and the surface web. The surface web is the easiest. That is the internet most people are used to using. One can find anything they need by using search engines like Safari and Bing. The deep web is a level more complicated. People are not always able to find things that are easily accessible on the surface web with the standard search engines. These tend to be things like government databases and online libraries. Then, we have the dark web. It is like the dark corner of a room, intentionally kept hidden with the use of normal search engines. This is where the Tor network is, which is why you can only access the dark web by using the Tor browser.

Being anonymous on the dark net is done by using the onion network. The standard internet directly accesses servers that are set up to host whatever website the user is visiting. When using an onion network, direct links are broken intentionally, and the data is sent through several pipelines or intermediaries before it gets to the final destination. The result is the same because you will ultimately reach the website you originally searched for. The medium through which the routes are transported is what prevents others from seeing who or what is behind the communication that was sent. Tor uses the onion router, and it is meant to be an anonymous and user friendly way to communicate with any operating system.

Originally, the dark net was invented by the US military. Law enforcement organizations, the government, and people in the military are some of the most common users of the dark net. They use browsers like Tor because the surface web makes it easy for others to see the near exact location of the user, even when the best encryption techniques are put in place. This is what helps protect agents who are out working in the field as well as politicians or soldiers in need of keeping their negotiations from being seen by others.

The dark net is also particularly popular with bloggers and journalists, generally those who are living in countries where censorship and the possibility of being imprisoned for political speech against said country are prohibited. Remaining anonymous online helps to keep all those people safe and allows them to communicate with other people as well as have access to information that may be blocked by firewalls. The dark net is also a platform for revolutionaries or activists who want to organize marches or protests without fear of retaliation from the government they oppose or revealing their location to anyone who may be watching.

Tor, which also stands for The Onion Router, is quite easy to access. It is also the most common platform used to access the dark net. If you are the kind of person who is technologically inclined, you can configure Tor to meet your specific needs. And if tech savvy is not something you are good at, that is okay too. Tor is easy for anyone to access and use. Tor is built on top of the Firefox internet browser, which most of us are familiar with already.

Tor gives its users added protection against government agencies who may be spying to collect information, traffic analysis and it also protects against hackers. Tor lets the user access sites that were purposely published with anonymity. Those are the most popular and frequently searched websites on the dark net.

A little earlier we briefly mentioned the Freenet Project, which is a browser similar to Tor. Through Freenet, one can create a private network in which any resource located or provided on the computer will only be accessible by those who have been placed on a list of friends. The I2P (Invisible Internet Project) is also similar in that it provides file sharing plugins, secure email servers, file storage and features geared toward social activities like blogging or chat.

Now, when you are ready to create your online persona, this is the place to let your imagination run wild. What is great about pseudonyms is you can call yourself whatever you like. If it is your intention to appear legitimate or conduct business using the dark net, you can also use a name that would be considered more common. Either way, you are free to do as you please. If you find yourself stuck, there are sites that can generate some interesting names on your behalf and you can almost guarantee it will give you a name that has not yet been used on the dark net. Whatever name you choose can be used for the email address, Bitcoins, or screen names on Tor.

Chapter 7

Tor Weaknesses

This is not what we want to think of when accessing a web that is supposed to be secure, but everything has a weakness, and we are going to cover the weaknesses of Tor so you can avoid them and feel safe using the dark net.

Like anything else in life, Tor has boundaries. It can provide protection against traffic analysis but cannot prevent the traffic from being confirmed. Some of the most common weaknesses are that of eavesdropping and below we are going to talk about the different kinds of eavesdropping.

The autonomous system, also known as AS, are segments used for exit or entry and relaying information for the destination site. Autonomous systems make it so traffic on those segments will interfere with communications between the end destination and the user.

Next, there is Exit Node Eavesdropping. Without being careful, the usernames, passwords, and Bitcoin information of the user can be intercepted if the person on the other end simply watches the exit nodes, which is where the data exits. Tor is unable to encrypt everything going out the exit node because the end to end encryption was never put in place. This type of eavesdropping does not breach the anonymity of Tor, but it does make it easier for people who may be watching to catch information on the exit nodes and use that information to decipher a location of the user. It can also be used for less nefarious reasons like traffic analysis, which simply aims to advertise to the user's likes and avoid their dislikes.

Another kind of attack is one we have mentioned a few times, and that is the traffic analysis. Advertisers get a peek at the traffic on the Tor network by looking at those exit nodes. They decide which ones to keep an eye on and use the information to advertise accordingly. It is not a malicious attack and is only meant to prompt the user to spend a little money online through their website. The traffic analysis also reveals the location of the user, and it can provide basic information like name and email or even phone numbers.

There is also the exit node push. This is where a person operating a site can choose to refuse data to enter the nodes. They can also reduce the number of users allowed on the network. An example of this is being unable to edit websites like Wikipedia through the Tor network.

Next, we have what is known as the bad apple attack. This is done through using BitTorrent while using the Tor network. A user's IP address can be revealed through

BitTorrent by taking advantage of Tor. The severity of the attack depends on the exit node control. On occasion, there could be a secondary attack so the user and their IP address or location can be fully exploited.

Another common attack is the exposure of the IP address. Through this method, there is a dissimulation technique that allows people to control the exit node. This was part of a research study that showed in twenty-three days there were three attacks that successfully exploited the system and revealed IP addresses.

Unfortunately, there are ways that Tor can be hacked, but the risk is minimal so long as you follow proper protocols.

Chapter 8

Staying Concealed While Using the Internet

There are quite a few ways to conceal yourself while surfing the web, a few of which we have discussed previously. There are some that are obvious such as the use of an incognito or private browser. There is another option that is less frequently discussed, and that is to kill cookies. This action does not kill supercookies, which we will discuss a little later, but it can keep your browsing anonymous while browsing the standard internet. One of the best ways to rid your computer of cookies is to use Ccleaner, a free downloadable program from the internet. It can delete flash and cookies.

You can also search anonymously by turning off the personalized search on whichever search engine you use. Whether it is Google or Bing, there is the option to turn off the search. You may have noticed when typing in the first few letters; most search engines will try to complete the sentence for you. That is the personalized search option. To turn this off, you will go to Search Tools then click on All Results and then Verbatim. This provides some anonymity, but not as much as it would if you used just the dark net. You can also choose to use search engines that are private, one of which we discussed earlier called duckduckgo.

You can also stop Google from tracking your location and keeping track of your searches. If you were not aware that this was happening, consider yourself informed. Google has so many options like calendars, Gmail, and Google plus that it can build profiles based on the services you use through its servers. Google uses a unified privacy policy which simply means that it can legally track you across any service. Unfortunately, that means they can scan emails, and it will use that data to personalize the ads from advertisers. Your profile photo can also appear on items you may have liked while you were logged into your Gmail account or Google Plus. This is something you can opt out of and is done by simply turning off all personalized ads. You are also allowed to download the Google Analytic Browser Add-on which will cease the collection of data based on the places you searched on the internet, which Google will later sell to their ad partners.

You are also able to block trackers on the internet. Each site on the web has cookies that are made just to track activity embedded in the site. Sponsored links, comment boxes, and ads are all examples of cookies that are embedded and used for tracking purposes. You can use anti-tracking plugins such as Privacy Badger, Ghostery, and Disconnect that are used specifically to block cookies made to track. This keeps analytic companies from building profiles based on the kinds of sites you visit while surfing the web. Any of those programs listed above are easily found and downloadable from the internet. Once they are put in place, they do the work for you and destroy tracking cookies before they even know what hit them.

There is also the option of a proxy network. Many of the options we have discussed in this chapter are great for dodging cookies but frequented websites, and online activity is still tracked by your browser's IP address. These IP addresses can help give an approximate location of the computer or tablet, and it lets the trackers know how often you go to specific websites. To get some more privacy, you can consider downloading the VPNs we talked about previously. There is another option known as CyberGhost, which is cheap and is compatible with PC, Mac, iOS, and Android.

Of course, there is the option to download an anonymous browser and is something that should be seriously considered. Plugins and proxies, as well as trying to recall whether you are using a private browsing session, can lead to a frustrating and extended web browsing environment. A lot of us get accustomed to using a certain kind of browser, and if that is something you can let go of, you can download a new browser as another option. Doing this allows the user to turn on their proxy networks with switches that are found in the toolbar. One of these is the Epic browser, which was modeled after Chrome. The privacy settings are incredibly high, and third party cookies are always blocked. Users can search whatever sites they like, and browsing is never tracked. You are going to see ads still, but the activity and sites you visit will not be logged. There is a neat counter on the homepage that will let you know how many times a tracker tried to log your activities in one day. It is a cool feeling to see that every attempt to track your activity was thwarted by the browser you use.

You can also consider services that provide data removal. There is a product called *DeleteMe* which costs around one-hundred dollars per year. That fee includes the deletion of all information collected by companies that will, in turn, sell it to other advertisers. The only pitfall to this is you must pay for it. Also, it does not necessarily remove every bit of information from the searches, which leaves the user slightly vulnerable.

While it is not common knowledge, you can hide your IP address by using an IP scrambler. One of the most common programs is called Virtual World Computing Cocoon. This will show the user as a *cocoon user* to those who may be spying. It is considered a smart proxy, and when logging into

Cocoon, the IP address on the site is the only thing that is seen, not the actual IP address of the person using Cocoon. This is a great service capable of protecting those who use Wi-Fi networks in public places.

You also have the option to disallow social networks to track your internet activity. Any time you click like on something on Facebook or Twitter, information on that is stored in massive databases and used to form ads based on your likes. If you would like to remove that from Facebook, you simply go to the privacy settings and click on adverts to control. By removing that option, the things you like on Facebook can no longer be tracked. Any social media site has this option, and unless you are unable to live without social media entirely, we strongly suggest you remove those options from all your social media outlets.

Because most of us are unable to completely stop using the internet or social media in general, this chapter has been geared toward finding other alternatives to browsing anonymously. This is for those using unsecured computers or tablets that have not got the option to download Tor. You will want to be able to use Tor to avoid being spied on while surfing the internet.

Chapter 9

Encryption and Supercookies

We briefly mentioned supercookies in the previous chapter, and this one is going to go over them in a little more detail. First, let us define what a regular cookie is. Unfortunately, we are not discussing the chocolate chip persuasion. HTTP cookies are known as a regular or simple cookie. It is code downloaded to a user's internet browser each time they reach a website. Those cookies can store information useful to the user, and the website can track interactions between the user and the website they reached. A good way to describe how this works is using Amazon to shop. Any item left in your cart are stored using a cookie so if you leave the website without making the purchase, those things stay in the cart for when you return. The cookie will send information to Amazon when you return to the site later.

Cookies are also able to let a website know the user is logged in, so the user does not have to input their login information repeatedly. The third-party cookies can track users across the internet and gather information to sell to marketing companies by simply letting them know what types of websites the user visited while online.

Now, a super cookie is like a tracking cookie, but it is much more complicated.

If you want to keep cookies from tracking your activity online, clearing the browsing history is a simple way to keep this from happening. It is a simple step and can clear every cookie that was previously stored on the computer. The only issue that creates is the user must input all their login information each time they visit, and any items left in virtual shopping carts will no longer be stored. That is good in that the cookies will not be able to track your activity but bad in that it causes extra steps each time you log in.

That technique will not work with the supercookies. They are not a standard cookie stored within the browser. There is information unique to the connection of the specified user that will be entered in the header of the HTTP by the internet service provider. That information can identify whatever website the user visited. Information between the server and the device being used means the user is unable to do anything about it. This information will not be stored on any device and hence cannot be deleted. Any ad blocking software mentioned is unable to block a supercookie.

Supercookies are particularly dangerous because of the violation of privacy that may occur. In general, cookies on any single website are not shared with another website. UIDH can be revealed to all websites, and that is where tons of information regarding internet searches, history and habits are stored. The supercookie is something that advertisers can use to find all deleted cookies from the device and then link them to new cookies.

The supercookie sounds like a mosquito that just cannot be killed. They can keep tons of information about your personal life and revive all the cookies you deleted that should not be stored on any of your personal devices. There is not much that can be done about the supercookie except to use VPNs. We talked about the top three previously, and in addition to using the Tor network, VPNs are a great added layer of security to keep those pesky cookies and supercookies from tracking and storing your activity and information.

VPNs work well on computers, but not handheld devices like smartphones or tablets, which tend to be at higher risk for supercookies. If you are using your phone to browse the internet, there is the option to use proxy settings that are encrypted. ISPs can remove that encryption, so you need to be careful to make sure they are in place each time you use your phone to browse the web.

It is an unfortunate fact that the options are limited when it comes to using your smartphone or tablet to search the web. Using an untraceable phone or avoiding using the

internet while on your phone are going to be your best bets,
even if they are difficult to imagine.

Chapter 10

Tor and Hacking

Hacking, in general, is considered illegal and yet is something done regularly through Tor as well as any other browser. Tor can be used to hack any application, but it is more difficult and requires slightly more patience. Hacking, in general, requires diligence and stealth as well.

Once you have downloaded the Tor browser (which undoubtedly you have by now), configure it in a manner that works best for you. Commonly Tor users simply allow Tor to set all the configurations through the setup process. If there is anything specific you wish to do during this process, there is undoubtedly a way to do so. Remember, anything done through the setup can be changed later to meet your needs.

As previously discussed, it is wise to test the network and ensure you are using Tor and not the standard web. To access the deep web, you will find deepweb.pw on the Tor URL bar. From there, you are going to be able to access services such as TorSearch, Hidden Wiki, and Tails.

Once you are in the deep Web, you can use those tunnels through Tor and access other websites that cannot be discovered on the standard web. Users are also able to add on tools to their browser that are going to be added layers of protection when it comes to activities on the dark net. The add-ons users are going to want to look for are Page Hacker and HackBar. Both of those are going to allow access to even deeper parts of the dark net.

Below are some steps for hacking into any system. The difference here is that it is being done through Tor and those add-ons we mentioned previously. Please note that hacking is an illegal activity. The purpose of this section is to simply be informative and should only be used for educational purposes.

1. Find the *nix terminal to use on all commands. Cygwin is one of the better programs and can mimic nix for users on a Windows system. (Remember that previously we stated Windows and Tor are not the best of friends. However, this is an alternative if Windows OS is your only option).

2. Ensure the computer that is going to be hacked is secure. Before starting, it is important to make sure your system is entirely secure, so a counter hack does not occur. Also, there needs to be little to no possibility that the person being hacked can trace the hack back to the user. Part of the reason behind this tutorial section is to enable the user to see if their own system is hackable. That is the

most legal way to check the security of your own system, and it is a neat technique to learn in the process.

3. Ensure the user has the ping utility tool so a target activity can be tested. There is a flaw in this tool in that the administrator of the system might be alerted and can shut the system down before any hacking takes place.

4. Scan the ports on the target system. There should be a list of all open ports provided from the ping tool in step three. In this step, the user is also going to be able to determine the kind of firewall in place in addition to the type of router used on the target system.

5. Ports like the FTP or HTTP are less protected and easily accessible or exploited. Open ports for LAN gaming are DUP or TCP and are also easier to access. From here the user is going to see SSH, which is secure shell service, running on the target system. On occasion, the user can force those ports open using brute force, which will allow access to them as well.

6. Finding the password. This is one of the more difficult steps, but this is also where brute force attack comes in. This will crack the password and allow access to the system.

These are the first steps used to hack into another system while in the Tor network. As hacking is illegal, these steps are general and meant to provide guidance to the user so they can ensure their systems are safe. It is not intended to hack into another system.

In this chapter, we are also going to provide some information on staying safe while using Tor as it seems fitting. Below are some precautions everyone should take to stay safe while using the dark net. Always keep in mind that while you are searching the net using Tor, there are authorities and hackers who are doing the same and they are attempting to discover who is hosting certain websites and what people may be accessing criminal sites as well. The basics are listed below.

1. First and foremost, use that pseudonym. You are going to want to remain as anonymous as possible. This cannot be stressed enough. Tor is used for anonymity so using your real information or profiles defeats the purpose of going to it all together.

2. Tor is slightly slow because of the sheer number of nodes that it must pass through. It is wise to use a VPN to give yourself that added layer of security when browsing the dark net.

3. Always disable scripts that are running. This is an option in Tor as well as any standard web browser. Most sites on the dark net are considered criminal, and if you

accidentally find yourself visiting one, the online authorities may want to try to track you down. Scripts were created with JavaScript, and as we previously discussed, Java or JavaScript should not be enabled while using the standard web let alone Tor. Those are meant to store things on your computer, which is exactly what using Tor is meant to avoid.

4. Always think twice before clicking links because they may not be what they appear or claim to be. Some of the search engines can appear misleading. Tor has its own search engines including duckduckgo, which we previously mentioned as well as Torch. If you are looking to research information and want to do so without worry, Tor has a library that is great for this purpose. That way you know you will avoid clicking into something you never intended. Inside the Tor library, you will also find tons of hidden search engines meant to add to the security and safety of using the Tor network. If this is your first time accessing Tor, the library is the best place to start.

5. Never download anything directly to your computer. This includes BitTorrents because they can provide the actual IP address for the user as it is meant to store things on a computer. That will make your activity traceable to you and can mean trouble if you are not careful.

Chapter 11

Using Tor to Avoid Marketers or Debt Collectors

At some point in our lives, many us have had the unfortunate pleasure of being indebted to collectors. Those debt collectors are particularly meddlesome and often call your place of employment or relatives just to try to track you down. Hiding from debt collectors is not going to dissolve the debt, and it is not an end all be all solution. It is simply a way to get relief from the harassing phone calls and incessant emails, so you have a moment to breathe and find a way to get yourself out of debt.

If it is difficult for debt collectors and marketers to find you, they will not be able to continue their harassment. One way to do this is to change your address. It is difficult to up and move, not to mention expensive. A way around this is to set up a PO Box. Always keep in mind that you are responsible for the debt that has been amassed. Once the PO Box in place, you can call all the creditors and change your address. They will try to ask for a physical address, but you are not legally required to give it to them.

Next, get yourself one of those disposable phones. They are cheap and have prepaid minutes. There is no contract requirement, and they can be bought anywhere from gas stations to Walmart. Because they are so cheap, you can have one for family and friends and another for those bill collectors. When you find yourself tired of all the phone calls, shut the designated bill collector phone off and take a moment to breathe.

Where does Tor come in, you ask? Right now. Earlier we talked about cookies and supercookies and all the activity that are traced on the standard web. Limiting your footprint online is a great way to hide from those collectors. You might be surprised to know that marketers and bill collectors look to social media accounts to find people. Refrain from posting personal information. Set all social media profiles like Facebook, Twitter, or Instagram to private. When doing this on Facebook specifically, anyone who is not a friend cannot contact you. Remember that pictures can speak a thousand words and provide clues as to where you may be. Photos taken on smartphones can also have the coordinates embedded in them, which might provide marketers or collectors with your geographical location.

If you apply for credit online, you will be required to give information like your physical address, social security number, and income. You can avoid risking this information being leaked by using Tor. The dark net is specifically intended to keep your personal information personal, and it is a great tool to use if you find yourself in need of applying for a line of credit. Unless you can avoid applying for credit in general, it is best to use Tor, so all information provided is kept private and not used for marketing.

Again, we previously discussed the importance of using the dark net to conceal activities and keep marketers from targeting you personally. To add that extra layer of protection, we implore you to consider the VPNs discussed in a previous chapter. The ideas discussed here will help to alleviate some of the stress but remember they are not fool proof.

Chapter 12

Using Tor to Avoid the NSA or Spies

One of the main government agencies dedicated to watching internet traffic is the NSA. They have people who keep an eye out for specific words or phrases that are meant to catch terrorists. While the clear majority of us are not using the internet for nefarious reasons, some of those words or phrases might be used without meaning harm at which point you may have caught the attention of agents of the NSA. Just like we do not want marketers or bill collectors to track us online, we certainly do not want to get the attention of the NSA. Using Tor is a great way to browse the internet without fear of accidentally saying something or using a catch word unintentionally.

Throughout this book, we have talked about added layers of security. Tor is not infallible, nor is there any other system out there that is. In addition to VPNs, users can use AsToria, which is a tool specifically for Tor which keeps prying eyes from seeing the type of information you are trying to access on the web.

AsToria was developed to allow Tor users a way to rid themselves of systems that will try to hack into the Tor network and reveal identities of those using the web anonymously. AsToria specifically works to fight against timed attacks against Tor. Algorithms were built into AsToria to protect against the worst-case scenario situations of cyber attack. AsToria consistently checks for and sends the user on the best and clearest route so they cannot be traced.

AsToria is an add on for Tor, just like the VPNs we discussed. In all honesty, while many government agencies use Tor, they would like to see it taken down for the common folk so they can easily see what everyone is doing online. They have tried several times to breach Tor and bring the network down and have not been successful. However, that is another reason to get those added security layers. It is one more wall any government agency would have to leap over to get to your IP address or geographical location. Any perceived weakness will be exploited, and Tor is designed to keep weaknesses at a minimum so its users can freely search whatever they please, post whatever political blogs they like and gather their fellow activists without fear of retaliation.

When used properly, Tor is perfectly capable of concealing your online activity. We briefly covered hacking in the Tor network, so users were aware it was a possibility. There will always be agencies or people looking to exploit others or simply see what they are searching for online.

For the most part, the NSA does not concern themselves with law-abiding citizens. So long as you are not continuously searching things on their watch list, there is nothing to worry about. We have all mistyped something and feared the worst, but no NSA agent ever came knocking on our door. They do have serious matters to attend to, which sometimes includes attempts at bringing down the Tor network.

Overall it is important to remember Tor is a wonderfully secret place you can go to search the dark net for things you might not be able to find anywhere else. It is intended to allow those types of searches as well as providing online anonymity to anyone who wishes to use it. Tor, in addition to the added layers of security, will make it easy for people to research or perform business transactions online without having to worry about their personal information being tracked and sold to the highest bidder. It is a wonderful invention for people simply wishing to exercise their right to browse freely.

Bitcoin

How to Get, Send, and Receive Bitcoins Anonymously

A Darknet Market Guide

Evan Lane

Introduction

The traditional method of using money, which is controlled by the banks or by the government, has been around for years. Most of us are familiar with using this form of money to get paid, make purchases, and more. But a newer form of currency, known as a cryptocurrency, has started to make waves all around the world as the best way to sell and make purchases in a secure and anonymous way. Bitcoin is at the head of this revolution and the number of people who use this currency, as well as the number of businesses that will accept this as payment, keeps on growing.

This guidebook is going to spend some time talking about the Bitcoin and how it has changed the way people do business. We will start out with some information about the Bitcoin and how it is different from other methods of currency. Then we will learn how to mine for Bitcoins, how to set up your account and remain anonymous online, how to accept payments for merchandise, and other ways to earn more Bitcoins, and even how to make your own payments using this currency.

Bitcoin has changed the way people accept payments and make purchases in a way that was not possible just a few years ago. Use this guidebook to learn more about how

Bitcoin works, how you can get started with Bitcoin of your own, and all the great reasons why Bitcoin is better than your current traditional currency for all your needs.

Chapter 1

What is a Bitcoin?

The Bitcoin is a new form of currency, but it works differently than the currency you are used to working with. This currency is created and held in the electronic world. There isn't a government or another entity that will control the Bitcoin, and it doesn't have a printed version. Rather, the Bitcoin is produced by people, and over time many businesses have gotten into this, helping computers to run all around the world. In fact, Bitcoin was one of the first examples of a new category of money called cryptocurrency.

How is Bitcoin Different?

While Bitcoin is a bit different than traditional currency, meaning you won't be able to print it off and it doesn't have a government or another entity that controls it, it can be used to make purchases like a traditional currency. You will be making these purchases electronically rather than taking the money to the store, but you can purchase goods you need online.

Some people prefer to use Bitcoin over the other currencies because it is decentralized. There isn't a single institute controlling the money and people are put at ease with this because it means a big bank isn't sitting there and controlling the money and how much it's worth.

No one is in charge of printing out the Bitcoin. Unlike traditional currency, this isn't a physical currency you can touch and use. Bitcoin is created and used digitally, and it is run by a community any person can join. To get more Bitcoins, you have to mine them, which happens by using a computing power in a distributed network. Inside of this network, you can also process the transactions made with this virtual currency, pretty much making it, so Bitcoin has its own network of payment.

So, Who Created Bitcoin?

Satoshi Nakamoto, a software developer, proposed the idea of the Bitcoin. He wrote out a mathematical proof that was able to handle this system of electronic payments and the whole idea was to produce a currency that was independent of any central authority. This currency can be transferred electronically, pretty much without any wait, and you will not have to deal with huge transaction fees.

The way Bitcoin is set up; you are not able to churn out as much of the currency as you want. The rules that make this Bitcoin currency work state there are only 21 million Bitcoins that can be created by the miners. However, you can divide up these coins, so they are in smaller parts, with the smallest amount being one hundred-millionths of the coin.

So, what has the Bitcoin been based off? When talking about conventional currency, it has been based on either silver or gold. In theory, you would be able to take your traditional currency to the bank, and you could get the value of it back in gold (you wouldn't be able to do this in reality, but it is the basic idea behind the currency). The Bitcoin is not going to be based on gold or silver like traditional currency, but it has been designed to be based on mathematics.

All around the world, there are a lot of people who are using the right software program that will follow the mathematical formula Satoshi Nakamoto designed to produce the Bitcoins. This formula is available easily, so it is possible for anyone to go in and take a look and create some of their own Bitcoins. The software is an open source code as well, so anyone can work on the code, make changes, and get it to work the way it should.

Some Characteristics of the Bitcoin

Outside of being a digital currency form you can create and use online, there are some main features of the Bitcoin that will help to set it apart from the traditional currencies. These features include:

It is a decentralized currency

The Bitcoin is not going to be controlled by just one central authority. All of the machines that mine the Bitcoins and take care of the transactions inside the system will create a network, and all the machines will work together. In theory, this means there isn't one central authority that will be able to mess around with the monetary policy and cause issues, or even an entity that can come in and take the Bitcoins away from you. Even if the network ends up going offline, your money will keep working.

The Bitcoin is easy to set up

When working with a traditional bank, it can sometimes be difficult to open a bank account. But with Bitcoin, you can set up your own address in just a few seconds, and there aren't a bunch of questions you have to answer. You are also able to avoid some of the fees that come with traditional banks, as there are none of these with setting up the Bitcoin.

Everything is anonymous

For the most part, you will be able to maintain some anonymity with this kind of currency. Users can choose if they would like to have one address or many of them, and the accounts aren't linked to any personal information like names or addresses, so you can go into the system without others knowing who you are.

There is transparency

While you can be anonymous when working in the Bitcoin system, the system is going to store the details of all the transactions that occur on the network. This information is going to be called the blockchain, and anytime you use a Bitcoin address publicly, anyone else will be able to tell the number of Bitcoins stored with this address and other information about the transactions. But even though they can see what is going on in your trading, they do not know who owns the Bitcoins so you can remain unknown in this system.

If you would like to ensure all things are as opaque as possible to avoid issues with people knowing who you are or keeping track of all your transactions, there are a few steps you can take. These include using different Bitcoin addresses and not sticking with the same one for too long and making sure you transfer the Bitcoin to just one address in Bitcoin.

Using Bitcoin can be fast

People love working with Bitcoin because it is a fast system you can use. While traditional currencies can take a few days or longer to transfer between two people and you just have to wait around for the currency to be processed before you can use it. But with the Bitcoin, you can send out the money to anywhere you would like, and it arrives there in just a few minutes. You have to wait only a few minutes for the Bitcoin network to process this payment, but it does arrive fairly fast compared to what you would see with banks and other traditional transactions. The good news is you won't be charged a lot of fees for using the Bitcoin system, even if you send money internationally.

How much is the Bitcoin?

Remember you can split up the Bitcoin a few times to share with others or to make the purchase you would like. This is because compared to other currencies, one Bitcoin can be worth quite a bit. For example, when you compare the Bitcoin to the United States Dollar, it is going to be worth $1,192.83 at the time of this book being published. When the Bitcoin is compared to the Euro, one Bitcoin is worth 1,134.84.

So, while you are only able to create 21 million of these coins, they are worth quite a bit of money for each one and are likely to be fine for a long time, especially considering there isn't a main bank that can mess with the system and run things into the ground. And the value of the Bitcoin has been going up as more people are trying to join the system, making it worth more than it was in the beginning.

Bitcoin is a great digital currency you can use to make digital purchases as needed. You get the benefit of a strong system that isn't based on a bank or a government who will make a mess of it, you can split it up into smaller units to make your purchases, and you will enjoy how fast it is to make the purchases without a lot of fees. We've now covered Bitcoin fundamentals. Let's look at how to start making your own Bitcoins.

Chapter 2

How to Mine in Bitcoin

After learning more about Bitcoin and all the benefits that come from this system, it is time to move on to learning how to get started. Mining in Bitcoin is the process of getting more Bitcoins to use on virtual products. When you are dealing with traditional sources of money, such as the United States dollar and the Euro, the government can print more money any time they need to. But since Bitcoin money never gets printed in the first place, you will need to *discover* it instead. There are computers all around the world which mine for these coins. Here we are going to take a look at the mining process for Bitcoin and the steps you should take to "discover" more of these coins for your own.

How Does This Take Place?

There are people all over the world who are using the Bitcoin network to send Bitcoins to one another, with the amounts varying based on what they are purchasing. But unless there was a record of these transactions, it is hard to figure out who has made the payments or not. The network for Bitcoin is going to work by collecting all the transactions that happen during a set period (such as a day or a week) and then placing all the information onto a list.

To keep track of all these different transactions that occur, the miner is going to be the ones who works to confirm all of these transactions. They will be able to take these transactions and then write them down into the general ledger.

How to Make a Hash of it

So, what is the point of this ledger? Why would the miner be so interested in writing out this information and keeping track of it all the time? This general ledger is basically a long list that consists of blocks known as the blockchains in this system. You can use it to explore all the transactions made between the Bitcoin addresses. You can watch a few particular ones you would like to keep track of inside of the network.

Any time a transaction shows a new block, it is going to show up on your blockchain. Of course, as time goes on, this list is going to get pretty long because it can show all the different transactions that took place over the Bitcoin network. A copy of this is going to be given to anyone who is participating in the game, so they all have an idea of what is going on.

But for this to work, the general ledger needs to be trusted, and it is all going to be left in a digital format. How can the users of Bitcoin be sure this blockchain is staying intact, and someone isn't coming in and tampering with it? This is where the most important job of the miners is going to come into play.

When a new transaction block is created, it is up to the miners to put it through a process. They will take the information inside the block, and put a formula to it so this information is going to be turned into something new. What this results in is something a lot shorter, and is going to seem random, and will include numbers and letters that are a hash. This hash is going to be stored inside of the block, somewhere near the end of the created blockchain, during some period of time.

You will notice there are some neat properties that come with these hashes. It is pretty easy to take the collection of data that creates the Bitcoin block and create a hash, but since the information is randomized, it is almost impossible to look at the data and figure out what it means. Each of the hashes you use will be unique, and they can take large data amounts and give them their own unique hash that hides the information while also making sure it doesn't match up to someone else. For example, you could change just one of the characters inside of a block, and the hash is going to end up as something completely new.

Mines are not using these transactions just to generate these hashes. They can use some other information in the data to help as well. One of the important pieces they will need to use is the hash that comes on the last block stored right at the end of the blockchain.

Because all the hashes in the block will be produced using the hash of whatever block was right before it, you are basically making it secure, such as a wax seal in the digital world. This system is going can confirm this block, as well as the other blocks that follow it, is legitimate because if someone comes in and tampers with it, everyone in the system would know.

If you were on the system and tried to fake out a transaction you were doing by changing one of the blocks already stored inside of the blockchain, you would notice that the hash of that block is going to change. If someone went through to see if the block was authentic by running and hashing the function, it is easy for them to find that the hash that you provide is different from the one that was stored on the system. They would see the changes, know the one on the blockchain is the right one and can tell your transaction is the false one quickly.

Because each of the hashes is used to help make up the hash that is going to be used in the following block, tempering with this particular block would mean the next block would have the wrong hash too. This would be a chain reaction that went all the way down the code, and it would make everything out of line.

The miners are responsible for keeping track of the different transactions that occur inside of the Bitcoin system. They use a randomized approach that will help to keep all of these secure and make it almost impossible for someone to go into the system and make changes without it being recognized. This is a great way to keep track of all the transactions happening inside of the system and helps to make it a pretty secure system to work with.

Competing to Get the Coins

Now that we know a bit more about working with the hashes and keeping the transactions safe, it is time to work on how each miner is going to be able to compete to get the coins. The miners are going to seal off a block with these randomized hashes to compete, using some software that has been designed to mine the blocks. Every time that you, as a miner, create a new hash successfully, you will be rewarded 25 Bitcoins.

This is a win-win for everyone. It helps everyone in the system to stay safe and secure from someone sending out false information to them or messing with the transactions, and it allows the miner who does this work to make some good money. This is the incentive given to the miners so that they keep on doing the work and the transactions will always continue.

The biggest problem with this is that creating a new hash from some data that you collect is not that hard and your computer can be good at getting this done if you choose to go with this method. The Bitcoin network has worked to make this a bit more difficult. Otherwise, everyone would go onto the system and make a lot of money in a few minutes by creating these hashes and the system would go a bit crazy.

The network for Bitcoin has introduced a process known as proof of work that has made it a bit more difficult to create these hashes so that all the Bitcoin is not mined in just a few seconds. The protocol in Bitcoin is not going just to accept any hash that you hand to it and there are certain rules that you will need to meet. First, you need to make sure that the hash looks a certain way such as having a set number of zeros at the beginning. Since there is no way to know how the hash is going to look like until you are done with it, it can be different. And if you add in some more data to the system, it is going to change up the hash of the whole thing.

As a miner, you will need to make sure you aren't meddling with the information inside the transaction data, but they are going to need to change some of the data that they use to make a brand-new hash. They can bring in another type of data, which is also random, to create what is known as a "nonce." This is going to be used along with the data inside of the transaction to make the hash. So, if your data isn't fitting in with the hash that the Bitcoin system asks for, the "nonce" is going to be changed so that the hash can change again. You can see how this could take quite a few tries to get it to work, but for those who are willing to keep on working on it and not giving it up, you can make some good money in the Bitcoin industry. The system will not give up over $25000 (if you converted from Bitcoin to USD) just for something that you could do in a few seconds, so these challenges are worth your time, but there is going to be some work that comes with it.

Hardware

There are three central types of hardware: GPU, FPGA, and ASIC. Mining was first done on general purpose central processing units (CPUs). As the processing was slow, miners advanced to graphics processing unit (GPU). Mining with graphic cards was easy to assemble, and the chip operated much faster. The term used to describe computer hardware that is configured to go faster than originally intended is overclocking. However, the GPU cooling system wasn't fast enough as the system is designed for video processing. GPU is created for complex calculations as found in video games and uses a lot of power. Eventually, the transition was made to Field Programmable Gate Arrays (FPGA).

This paved the way for Application Specific Integrated Circuits (ASIC) mining. ASIC are chips specifically created for mining. They are more advanced and use less energy than other hardware. Examples of hardware are Avalon 6, AntMiner S7, and AntMiner S9.

Bitcoin Cloud Mining

Another alternative to owning your hardware is to obtain contracts for Bitcoin cloud mining. With this option, you do not control the physical hardware. Select the best hardware for you. Be very aware that there has been a huge number of cloud mining rip-offs. If you're unsure of some of the names I will list some for you so you can familiarize yourself with some of the service operators. Examples include Bitcoin Cloud Mining, Genesis Mining, Hashing 24, Minex, Hashflare, Eobot, MineOnCloud, Hashnest, Minergate, and NiceHash.

Choosing Your Hardware

You must consider two main factors when choosing your hardware:

1. Hash Rate

2. Electricity

The hash rate is the measurement at which your hardware completes an operation. The measurement of the rate is megahashes, gigahashes and terahashes per second. The higher the rate, the greater is the possibility of cracking a transaction block. Research and make comparative notes before selecting your hardware.

The other factor is energy consumption. Calculate the amount of hashes you will receive for each watt. To calculate this, divide the hash count by the number of watts.

Estimate the effectiveness of your miner by checking on a mining profitability calculator. There are several available on various websites so make use of one. You can insert data like hash rate, energy consumption, the price of equipment and the current bitcoin cost to determine the length of time it will take to see a return on your investment.

There are professional mining centers such as BitFury Mining Center located in Georgia. The company has offices in other locations such as in Hong Kong, London, Amsterdam, and Iceland. Another mining rig is Avalon ASICS. The parent company of Avalon ASIC is Canaan Creative. The company's owner established Avalon in 2012 and customers are satisfied with the company's record.

Many people preorder from mining rigs, and it can be very frustrating when it takes a long time to receive your Bitcoin miner. The longer it takes, it diminishes your mining time. Butterfly Labs was launched in 2010. By 2014 customers had many complaints about the company. Miners grievances included paying in advance for high-speed equipment only to get them much later than agreed. Individuals received damaged machines, and in many instances, they never received any machine at all. Eventually the government intervened after so many complaints were filed. Do proper research about the company and the waiting time before making your order.

If you wish to operate a center, you must factor in the cost of electricity, the speed of the network and climate. The colder it is, the better it is for you to cool your center. Iceland is one cool place for mining.

Whether to Operate Solo or As A Group

If you're a novice and not sure about your next move, these factors are what you should consider. Is mining lucrative for you? Bitcoin mining is comparable to the gold rushes of yesteryear. There will be challenges. Various factors determine your profits. Functioning as a miner utilizes much electricity. So, you should know the rate to determine your profitability.

It will be prudent for you to join a mining pool as collectively as a group it will be more cost effective. Members receive profits according to the productivity. You will need a mining calculator. Insert the data on the miner you wish to purchase and ascertain the length of time needed to obtain a profit or break even. Know what best suits you.

Payment for mining can be pay-per-share or proportional. In the former model, i.e., pay-per-share a flat fee is rewarded for each share above a particular level of complexity. The latter model is based on the proportion of work. There are other models, but the objective will be to ensure that you agree with calculation. Currently, though the tendency is to operate as a group rather than solo, take note of what is known as pool hopping. This is explored later.

Software

If you are mining in a pool, make sure that you agree with the Bitcoin network rules. Ensure that the other miners share the same principles as you. You will also need outstanding connectivity to receive updates quickly. If you work solo, know the challenges of mining for a long time before earning.

Mining software for Mac OSX, Linux and Windows include CGMiner, BFGMiner, EasyMiner, and MinePeon. You can get extra applications from those listed above as well as BitMoose, 50 Miner, BTC Miner, Pyminer, and Ufasoft Miner. The list is not exhaustive. New models have certain presets such as your bitcoin address, which is something you'll need.

You have your hardware and software. Your next move is to register for a Bitcoin wallet. Your bitcoin wallet stores two keys. The public key for other people to send you bitcoins. The other key is the private key, and that must be safeguarded. Your private address enables you to spend bitcoins. If you lose it, you won't be able to recover it, and your funds will be gone forever.

There are various kinds of wallets available. It is advisable to back it up and keep it safe. These are the various categories:

- Hardware
- Paper
- Desktop
- Web
- Mobile

Hardware Wallet

Hardware wallets are a safe hardware device created to store private keys. Some of these hardware wallets are Trezor, Ledger, and KeepKey.

Paper Wallet

It is a document with all the information to obtain Bitcoin private keys. Individuals prefer this method as the most secure way. Other miners may prefer to store their wallets on their computer. That can be risky if there isn't any encryption. If you select a paper wallet, there are no chances of you being robbed of Bitcoins if someone hacks or sends a virus to your computer. It's comparable to having a personal safe with all your valuables tucked inside of it. Your valuables can only be stolen if someone goes with the entire vault. A vault is not something someone can easily open or just lift out of your home. They would have to know the combination. Paper wallets is an ideal option for those individuals who are more concerned about having long term savings.

You create your keys offline, print on paper and secure it offline. To create private keys offline follow these steps. Visit the website BitAddress.org in your browser. Insert a USB Zip drive and save the web page. Remove the drive and switch off the internet. Restart your computer with a clean boot. This step is a simple cautionary step that allows you to make sure that you have no spyware.

Keep the internet off when you're restarting your computer. Insert your drive and double click on the web page. It will appear in your browser. Select the tab that says Paper Wallet. Print as many paper wallets as you like. This is advisable, so in the future, you can add any amount on each one. You will notice there is a part that says Bitcoin address and another part that says Load & Verify. Next to it is a QR code that can be scanned. On the other side, you will see a part that says Private Key and the word Spend. This part has a QR code also.

The Bitcoin address is printed on it. Your next step is to send funds to the address. Your private key is not online. It is as if it never existed for it cannot be traced. Be very careful with your paper wallets for if your discard them by accident, you are not only throwing away your wallet but the money as well. Safely store it in a bank safety deposit box, a special drawer, a vault in your home or any safe place.

You can take screenshots of the address just in case of an emergency and store it on a USB drive. Encrypt the information, so if someone accesses your drive or steals it, your information is safe.

Desktop Wallets

Desktop wallets are also known as software wallets. They are wallets which you install on your computer. I'm sure that you've had a computer crash before or limited functionality of your computer. Therefore, if this happens and you lose your data, then the Bitcoin stored on your computer will also be lost.

Also, you must be aware that your wallets become susceptible to computer viruses, spyware, and malware. To secure this type of wallet, you must encrypt it. You will have to enter a password every time you use your wallet as it holds your private key. Realize also that hackers can crack codes by logging your computer key strokes.

You can store your Bitcoins on your desktop, but for larger sums, you also have the option of storing them on paper wallets.

Some software wallets which you can use are Armory, Bitcoin -Qt, Multibit, and Electrum. Amory has improved security and is one of the longstanding desktop wallets. If you use this, you will have to download the whole blockchain on your computer. You'll be private as it doesn't disclose the IP address connected to your wallet.

Electrum is one of the preferred wallets as it is convenient. It's simple to install, and you do not have to download the complete blockchain. You can also use additional plugins and add-on.

Web-Based Wallets

Web-based wallet which is also referred to as an online wallet safeguards your keys. However, it is on a computer that another individual operates. Some of these online services allow you to connect your mobile and desktop wallets. Examples of some of these organizations are Coinbase, Circle, and Strongcoin.

From a security standpoint, the website you choose provides you with the code to run on your mobile app or browser, and it stores the keys. Preferably the website would encrypt the keys with a password that you alone should know. If you have trust issues, then this option is not for you. You will have to entrust the website that the code delivered does not release your key or password.

Owning an online wallet is very convenient as you do not have to install anything on your computer. On your phone, you install the app. On the other hand, if the individuals who operate the website are not trustworthy or if a malicious person comprises the site, your bitcoins will be at stake.

Mobile Wallets

If you prefer to keep things on your phone, for convenience, then get a mobile wallet to store your private key. You can download a subsection of the blockchain, to accommodate your phone's memory space. You use an app to access your web wallet.

Securing Your Wallet

Various ways to keep your wallet protected are:

- Encryption
- Backing up. For information stored on your computer, back up your files on an external hard drive or drives. There is the option of online backup systems. Again, be

careful with this selection as the information will be online.

- Multi-signature
- Take it offline

For this purpose, we will use Coinbase as an example of setting up an address:

You will go to the website to sign up. Enter your first and last name in the correct boxes. Give your email address and select a password. Once you agree to the User Agreement and Private Policy, create your account.

To obtain an address, sign in with your email and password. Create your address. You can create however many addresses you want. When you select the details tab next to an address, you will see the QR code. This is like barcodes that anyone can scan to get the bitcoin address.

Select the Best Option

Before selecting a wallet, first, determine what activity you will engage in. For example, if it will be for long-term investing, a paper wallet is better. If you want to buy Bitcoins at a low rate and sell at a higher rate, your focus is more on short-term investing. As a result, you can consider a desktop wallet. If you are more interested in a prompt money exchange, a mobile wallet and web wallet are suited for your needs.

You do not have to limit yourself to one wallet. Always ensure that you take precautionary measures as discussed, regardless of whichever wallet you chose.

Mining Pools

These are some factors to consider before joining a mining pool:

- What method is used for payments? Methods include proportional, pay per share, pay per last N shares, and score based.
- How often do miners find a block?
- What is the charge to mine and withdraw funds?
- Is it a simple or a difficult process to withdraw funds?
- Is the pool settled and established?

Choose a mining pool of your choice and set up an account to receive a username and password. Simply visit the website link of your choice. Select the Sign Up Here tab and complete the instructions provided. Next, select Worker. For every worker you operate, you will need a worker ID to track all your work that you've done. In other words, you can have many workers for every portion of mining hardware you utilize.

Mining Strategies

Some miners transition between various pools. This term is called pool hopping. Let us assume that pool A payment model is pay-per-share and pool B model is proportional. For someone who wants to pool hop, one must know when is the ideal time to switch. When the expected rewards from one pool are high, you stay in that pool. Switch to the other when the returns are low.

GHash was one of the most popular mining pools years ago. The pool was so populated that in 2014 it had an estimated 51 % of the total Bitcoin miners grid. Miners flocked to this pool as GHash offered good incentives. Eventually, the company no longer allowed new miners to join the pool. In choosing your pool research properly. Compare the deals offered by various pools. There are transaction fees and other related fees so make your comparison.

GHash owned the largest pie of the mining pool in 2014, but a year later other pools became more popularized. GHash no longer topped the charts. Names of high ranking large mining pools are AntPool, BTCC Pool, F2Pool. Other pools include BC Monster, Give Me Coins and Multipool.

Things to Consider

If you are new to mining, take these factors into consideration:

- You decide what deals to include in a block. The usual approach is to take account of any transaction that has a higher fee.

- You choose on top of which block to mine. The standard approach is to develop the longest valid chain.

- When two distinct blocks are revealed at the same time, there will be a 1-block fork. Either block is acceptable. The standard approach is to build on top of the block that you first became knowledgeable of.

- You control when you reveal new blocks to the network. Usually, it is announced right away, but you can delay publicizing it if you prefer.

I have highlighted what the normal behavior is. However, there will be times when opting to choose a different strategy works best in your favor. It depends on your mining practices.

Forking Basics

Forks occur when two miners discover a block at the same time. Other blocks are added to one block so that it becomes the longest chain, and the other block is abandoned.

Another way in which a fork can happen is when developers modify the software rules to determine the validity of a transaction. When a block has transactions that are not valid, the network abandons the block. As a result, the miner who found the block stand to lose the reward.

Hard Fork

A hard fork is the term used when there is a software development that changes the rules. The new software would validate blocks that were once invalid by the old software. It becomes an issue when a part of the network prefers to adhere to the old rules.

Soft Fork

This is when there is a change to the rules so that it goes backward. There becomes a restraint on valid transactions. As a result, the old version receives the block, and the new version does not.

The issue with forks are raised for as a miner you will have to pay attention to the rules of the community as to what validates a transaction and the contents of the block chain.

Strategies

The standard assumption is that everyone will be honest. The reality is that other practices are involved in mining. There is the practice of selfish mining. This is the term given when a pool makes extra money at the risk of negatively affecting the system.

Selfish Mining

This is when miners keep information about the blocks they discover. Miners only release the information when necessary. Let's assume that F discovered blocks before other miners. They mine on top of what they perceive to be the longest chain. When they have found a valid block, then F can declare the blocks he had secretly kept. F blocks would be the longest valid chain. The block that the other miners spent much time discovering would be abandoned. F does this to obtain more mining rewards. This is very disadvantageous to other miners as they would have used their resources.

After considering the resources that miners have vested only to realize they lose instead of gaining, some miners change their behavior. Miners who were once open and truthful may be lured into becoming selfish miners. Such practices harm the community and reduce revenues of miners. For some miners, principles pale in comparison when rewards are the main focal point.

Mining Bitcoins can be a great way to make some money on the system if you would like to work with coding and end up with a challenge. If you are good at making some of these, you can make quite a bit of money, and it is much faster than you would find with some of the other methods on this website. Since there are so many different transactions that go on inside of this network, there are a lot of opportunities to work with this, but for someone who is trying to get into the Bitcoin life and who likes a bit of a challenge, mining Bitcoin could be the option for you.

Chapter 3

How to Use Your Bitcoin and Still Remain Anonymous

One of the big reasons that people choose to work with Bitcoin rather than the traditional forms of currency is that they want to remain anonymous. In our modern world with all the technology around us, it is common to worry about someone getting ahold of the information that comes with your transactions, such as your name and address, and use it for their own goods. But with Bitcoin, you have the option to remain anonymous with your transactions, even the person you send the money to for purchases doesn't have to know who you are for it to go through.

Some people have tried a lot of different options to remain anonymous online. But if you must make some purchases online, it becomes hard to make them and get everything to go through when you use a pseudonym. Bitcoin is the solution that you are looking for because it makes it hard for someone to be able to get your information, for people to compare your online persona and your real-life personality, and it is going to help you keep your information safe.

There are a few steps you will need to take to set up your Bitcoin account, so you can use it and keep some of the anonymity that you want when making purchases online. The steps you need to get started on the Bitcoin environment, communicate with others on the system, send and receive Bitcoins, and even browse the web anonymously include:

Step 1:

First, you need to get Tails and download it. This is something you can find on the Linux operating system, and you can get it on a USB stick and DVD. The nice thing is that you won't need to install this onto the computer, helping to keep things more secure. Tails will come with all the software that you will need pre-installed onto your USB stick. Once you get this set up, you can route all your traffic through the Tor network that should be created. There are a few ways that you can get the Tails software, either from a friend who is willing to share or from the Tails website. It is not too hard to deal with Tails, you do need to go through and manually install the program with the instructions provided.

Step 2:

Now that the software is ready to use, it is time to fire up Tails. If you downloaded this from the website, you can click on the ling, or you can insert the USB or DVD to get it all started. If the program is causing some difficulties, you can go through with the BIOS startup, and if you already have a persona that you like to use, you can use this as the way to access Tails. If you want to remain anonymous, you need to make sure that no personal information is showing during your chats with some of the other users, documents, and transactions. Always keep the browsing that you do during this process focused and always be careful about logging on to some of your social media accounts when you are on the Tails program.

Step 3:

For this step, it is time to enable a program called "persistence." This is an important step because you need to have this part of the program ready to go if you would like to save information into the Tails system. You may notice that there is a heading called Applications that you should click on. From here, you can select on Tails and then choose which option you would like to configure.

If you want to make sure that this option is going to work, you should use the USB drive to create a program for the Tails Installer. If you worked with this stick manually, it is important to copy the Tails using a completely different USB drive. The Tails installer process will be easy to find by going to Applications, Tails, and then Tails Installer. From this location, you can pick out the passphrase that you would like to use. Make sure it is something that you can remember, and that it is secure because you will be using this each time that you get on the Tails system.

During the installation process, Tails is going to ask what information you wish to store on the system. If you want to keep the connection secure, it is critical that you don't store a lot of information on Tails, but you can store as much or as little as you would like. This also means that you will need to remember what items are set up to use in Tails and you need to set them up every time that you are logging into the service. You can make the decisions for what goes on the software, but it is recommended that you save Network Connections, Browser Bookmarks, GnuPG, Personal Data, and Bitcoin inside of this system.

Once you have chosen which items you would like saved to the Tails system, you need to restart Tails, making sure that persistence has been enabled. Once the system all comes back up, you can enter the passphrase to get back one. Anything you do within your persistence folder can be saved if you want to shut down the computer.

Step 4:

Now it is time to set up your KeePassX. If you want to use the Dark Net, you will need this extra piece. It is going to

store your passwords of all your accounts, so you just need
to remember one or two rather than all of them. You can
find the KeePassX under applications, then accessories,
and then KeePassX. You must create a new password that
goes to this database, and you can do this by clicking on
File and then Create New Database.

Inside, you can find a program known as Diceware that
helps you create a longer password that is good for security
but is also easy to remember and helps you to access the
KeePassX. This password will be the second one out of
three that you should remember to make this system work.
All three of the passwords created from then on out are
going to be stored inside of KeePassX to make things
easier, and you can find them inside of the persistent
folder.

Whenever you would like to create a brand-new password,
you can just click on the yellow key, and it will ask if you
will add a new entry. Give the password a title and then
enter in the information needed. The button you really
need to pay attention to is the Gen button, which will be on
the right of your Repeat field. You can click on this button
to create a brand-new password. You can choose some of
the specifics of the password, such as how long you would
like it, what special characters are needed, and more.

To make sure that you are getting the best security out of this method, don't even look at the password given to you. Just pick the settings that you want for the password and then let the system create one for you. It will automatically be saved inside of KeePassX, and you can just pull it up when needed, without needing to know it yourself, and if someone happens to look over at the screen when the password is being placed in, all they would see are some symbols and not the word. Once the password is created, you can just copy it before pasting into whichever site you need to get access to.

Step 5:

The next thing that you will need to do is work on the PGP Key. Inside of Tails, you can make up a brand-new PGP key, which is found inside of Applications and then Utilities before clicking on Passwords and Keys. At this point, you need to look for the symbol that looks just like a blue plus sign, right beneath the GnuPG key.

Once you have clicked on the right button, you need to enter your email address and name, making sure to use the pseudonym you created if you want to send off encrypted emails and you want to make sure no one knows your identity. The password for this section is required every time you are working on file decryption, or you have an email sent to you and which is encrypted.

Step 6:

From here, you can set up the program Electrum. You can get onto your Bitcoin Wallet (which we will talk about a bit later) and then click on Applications. From here you can click on the Internet and then Bitcoin Wallet. You can think of Electrum as a lightweight wallet in Bitcoin, and you will not need to use a copy of blockchain to make this work since you can rely on other node types. If you would like a chance to see your balance in here, you just need to type in the right Bitcoin address right to the Blockexplorer.

So, when you are ready to make your own wallet, you need to be inside of the Blockcypher, which is also the area where you can keep track of your transactions and your balance. There isn't any need for you to use anything other than your standard wallet since this is going to work out just fine. Inside, there are going to be thirteen English words that will be the representation of the wallet seed. Anyone who has that same seed combination will be able to get into the wallet and still Bitcoins so make sure that you store these thirteen words in a place that you can find but no one else can get to.

Once you have the password all set up, you can press the proceed button so that you can put the wallet seed shows up in your window. Now choose your password, using KeePassX to help store this and to create a good password that is hard to remember. You can use this password with all your transactions, and once this is all set up, you can get and send payments with Bitcoin as often as you want. If you would like to have a few different things linked up under your account, you can create a different wallet to help keep things more anonymous, whether you have different accounts or you would like to have one for a single transaction. If you keep these wallets separate, it becomes easier to separate out your money for your privacy and accounting purposes.

Step 7:

Now that you have gotten all of this setup, there may be times when you would like to communicate with this program. This is completely possible when you use the OTR and the XMPP to do the communication. Pidgin is the best program to use when you want to have communication with some of the other users. One issue that comes with this is that you must be online to get your messages through this program, but otherwise, it is an easy to use system that will keep your identity safe.

It is pretty easy to install the Pidgin system. You just need to visit Applications and then Internet before clicking on Pidgin. After here, you will be able to access the Pidgin site by adding your account and then checking that you want the MPP to be your protocol.

You can choose what kind of search engine you would like to use for this to keep things simple. You can then choose a password (which you can use with the KeePassX again, so you don't have to remember all the passwords). Make sure you are clicking on the box that says "create new account on the server." After you click on the right box, you need to close the window before reconnecting again so that a new account for chat is enabled inside of Pidgin.

Once your window opens up again, your system is going to ask you for your password and your username, something that KeePassX can help with if you don't already have some of these setup. When you are ready to work on this chat function, you can click on your encryption option that says OTR. You will be able to do this easily by clicking OTR and then Start Private Conversation. You also have the option to verify the integrity of your chat by clicking on OTR and then on the button to Authenticate Buddy.

Step 8:

We have already done a lot of cool things that you can do with Bitcoin, but now we are going to learn how to back up the information that you are using inside of Tails by using the PGP system. This one is going to take the most work out of all the steps, so be ready to put in some effort. You want to put in some effort to lock up the key so that accessibility to it is hard and you won't have to worry about someone getting your information. You can create a password that is strong when you use Diceware to go with your PGP key.

The key that you are going to be using can be loaded onto any USB device, and then you should deposit it with someone who can guard it well for you. You may also want to consider having a regular backup of your documents, such as hard copies or another location so that nothing bad happens if there is some loss.

So, when you are ready to do a backup, you need to select all the folders and files that you would like to save. Then you can right click on your selections and then click on encrypt. In some cases, a popup window is going to show up, asking which of the keys you are interested in encrypting. From this location, you just need to select on your PGP key. When in this step, make sure that you avoid clicking on your sign options. When you are ready to decrypt one of the stored files, you will just need to find the file that has the .gpg label, double-click on it, and then place in the password that you used for the PGP key.

Step 9:

At this point, you have created a good account, with quite a bit of anonymity attached to it, for just one of your accounts. But many people choose to have multiple accounts on Bitcoin to avoid causing issues, to keep their information private from others, and even to protect their identities. It is fine to have more than one account, but you do need to make sure that you are repeating the steps in this chapter to make sure that all the accounts have the same safety features in place.

When repeating these steps, you need to make sure that each download of Tails has a different USB drive to handle the pseudonyms that you are creating. Each of the sticks needs to have different information as well, such as different keys for PGP, a different database for the KeePassX, and even different passwords to keep things safe and secure.

Chapter 4

Getting Your First Bitcoin

Once you get your Bitcoin account set up, it is time to get some Bitcoin. You will need to have these to help make the purchases that you would like, to do some investing, and for other purposes. Now, you could choose to start accepting Bitcoin from your customers with the product or service that your business sells, but if you just want to have the Bitcoin to make a purchase, you need to make sure you have some Bitcoin to start. Let's look at the steps for exchanging some of your regular currency to Bitcoins to get started with this great currency.

Pick Out an Exchange Service

The first thing that you should do is find an exchange that you feel comfortable with. This is one of the easiest ways to get ahold of the Bitcoin. A Bitcoin exchange is going to work just like any other currency exchange that you would like to use. You can register for an account and then take any currency that you are using and have it converted in real time to Bitcoin. There are hundreds of these exchanges that you can use, and you can pick the one in your area or which accepts your form of currency. Some of the most common currency exchange services for Bitcoin include:

- CoinBase: this one is great when dealing with Euros and US dollars. The company has made it easy to do your buying and trading because it has options for online and mobile app conversion.
- Circle: this service is going to offer you the chance to exchange, receive, send, and store your Bitcoins. This one is only available to those who are inside the United States, and you will need to hook up your bank account to this service.
- Xapo: this is a debit card provider as well as a wallet for Bitcoin. It will help you to make deposits of your personal currency that you can convert over to Bitcoin and use inside of the account.

There are also some exchange services will make it easy to trade in your Bitcoins. Other ones are going to act as a wallet service that will give you some selling and buying capabilities, but these are going to be a little limited. Most of the wallets and exchanges will store amounts of the digital currency for you to make things easier, similar to what you find with your regular bank account. These are some of the best options for exchanging your regular currency to get some Bitcoin.

Provide Some Proof of Identity

While you can work inside of Bitcoin as an anonymous person, you do still need to show some proof of who you are to get started. When you are ready to sign up for one of the exchange services listed above (or one of the other ones), it is important that you provide some personal information to create the account. Most countries require that you show this personal information to any financial systems so that the users aren't hiding money for taxes or to prevent issues with money laundering.

Use Your Exchange Accounts to Purchase the Bitcoins

Now that you have given proof of your personal identity as well as set up the exchange account that you would like to use, it is time for you to get the money into the account so that it can become Bitcoin. At this point, you will need to link on one of your bank accounts to the Bitcoin so that the funds can move from the bank account over to your new account for the Bitcoin. This is often going to be done with a wire transfer that can sometimes include a small fee to get it done.

One thing that you may want to try to keep your money safe is to have a separate account for using your Bitcoin. You can put some money in the account any time that you want to switch it over to Bitcoin. This keeps the money safe in case someone gets into your exchange account since there isn't going to be any extra money in that account once you do the switch.

There are some exchanges that will make it easier to make some deposits in person to the bank accounts. You can go to the bank and do this all face to face, compared to doing it with an ATM as the other methods require.

If the exchange is asking you to link your account to it, it is likely that you will only be able to use a bank from the same country as the exchange service. This means that if the exchange service is in the United States, you will need to have your bank account be located this country to be able to use it. There are a few exchanges that will allow you to move your money to accounts overseas, but you should know that there are fees associated with this and it often has a longer delay compared to choosing a bank account in your local country.

Find a Seller

The next step for you to try out is finding a seller who will sell their Bitcoins to you. The best site to use is LocalBitcoins because it allows you to find someone who is in your area who wants to sell their Bitcoins. You will be able to meet the seller face to face and negotiate the price that you will pay for the Bitcoins. This site and some of the others that you can work with will have an added layer of protection in place for both parties.

For those people who aren't that comfortable meeting up with people face to face, or you are in an area where you can't find anyone who is willing to sell their Bitcoins, it is a good idea to use a site like Meetup.com. This is when you find a group of people who would like to purchase Bitcoins and then as a group you will decide who to purchase the Bitcoins from.

Before you meet up with someone to make the purchase, it is important to decide on the price that you will pay for the Bitcoins. You should always check the rates for the Bitcoin before meeting up so that you know how much you should be paying. You may need to pay an additional premium of up to 10 percent since you are meeting with the person. You should check with the seller to know if they want you to pay for the Bitcoins in cash or with online payment options. Some sellers would rather go with cash or another payment form that is non-reversible to keep it safe, but some are fine with options like PayPal. A good trader is going to be willing to negotiate the price with you before you get started and they will want to meet up quickly so that no dramatic shifts happen with the price of the Bitcoin.

When you meet with the Bitcoin seller, make sure that it is in a public place to keep both of your healthy. You should also have some method to access the wallet for Bitcoin, either through a laptop, tablet, or a smartphone. You will be able to use these to make sure that the transaction has been processed. Make sure this happens before you pay the seller, or they could take off with your money, and you won't be able to find them.

Using an ATM for Your Bitcoins

Another option that you can use is an ATM to access your Bitcoin. There are several ATMs available specifically for the Bitcoin, and while it is a new concept, this is something growing all the time as Bitcoin becomes more popular. Going online and finding a Bitcoin ATM map is the best way to find out if there is one of these near you and where it is located. You can find these at other banks familiar with Bitcoin or many universities around the world.

For the most part, the Bitcoin ATMs that you are going to use will only accept cash. Since you are only using Bitcoin in these, you will not be able to use credit or debit card transactions. So, you can find one of these ATMs and take out some cash from your account when you need to.

You are also able to insert some cash into one of these ATMs to make sure that you can get it into one of your accounts. You can then scan your QR code or your wallet, or you can use the access code for your account through your smartphone. This is going to make it easier to load some Bitcoins into the wallet online. Keep in mind that the exchange rates for these ATMS is going to vary and they will have not only the standard exchange price that you are used to, but also another 3 to 8 percent on top of that. This is going to cost you a little bit more to complete compared to using the online sources, but if you are in a hurry to get it to work, you can change out your cash for Bitcoins in this manner.

There are many ways to get the Bitcoins you need to start making purchases or do some of the other options. Some people choose just to get started with their own store or with mining to get Bitcoins for free. However, if you are looking to get started with lending or even to make some purchases at stores that accept Bitcoin, you need to have a method of getting ahold of these first. Working with a seller, exchange or your local Bitcoin ATM are good places to start. Keep in mind that the cost of the Bitcoins that you want to use will vary based on how much money you would like to spend as well as the current exchange rate based on the type of currency you are using to make the purchase!

One of the largest Bitcoin exchanges was a Japanese company called Mt. Gox that was established in 2010. By 2014 it was managing numerous Bitcoin transactions, and eventually, Bitcoin withdrawals were suspended. It was later revealed that customers and the company's Bitcoins were stolen. They were valued at an estimated amount of $350 million. In the end, the company declared bankruptcy. In January 2015, there was a decrease in the value of bitcoin.

One of the effects is that since the fall of Mt. Gox exchange, the level of centralization has decreased. Greater security measures have been implemented, and users have become more adept at trading. One valuable lesson is to avoid keeping funds inside an exchange if you can't afford to lose it.

Two years later, Bitfinex, another company took a massive blow as an estimated $66 million worth of Bitcoins went missing. Additionally, Bitcurex, a Polish exchange also reported the theft of Bitcoins due to a hack that occurred in October 2016. I'm using these as examples to show you the risks involved. Engage in proper due diligence checks when selecting your platform.

Various fees involved:

- Fiat deposit
- Fiat withdrawal
- Bitcoin deposit
- Bitcoin withdrawal
- Transactions fees

Things to consider:

- The timeframe to validate every transaction as the

exchange rate may change during the waiting period. Depositing legal tender currency (fiat currency) can take time such as more than a week.

- The different validations that are necessary.
- Various exchanges have fees, and you should make comparisons.
- Price differences.

Chapter 5

Making Purchases with the Darknet Marketplace

One option that many people are interested in searching for and using their Bitcoins on is the Darknet market. This is also known as the cryptomarket, and it is a commercial website that works on platforms like I2P and Tor. They are going to be similar to a black market, but they will work online rather than in person. Since this is a market that often has illegal products for sale, using the Bitcoin can be a great way to get the products you need without anyone having an idea of what you would like to use. These have become popular recently, and according to a study that was done at the University of Portsmouth, these darknet markets are now at the top of the list of popular Tor websites visited.

On the darknet, you will find that transactions are going to be done with Bitcoin as the payment to make sure that both parties can remain anonymous to protect their identity. Also, tumblers are added to the mix, and a secure PGP is put in place to make sure that the communication between the vendors and the buyers are safe from outside eyes.

There are many things you can purchase on the darknet, not all of which are illegal, and you can use the anonymity that the Bitcoin provides you to make these purchases in a safe and secure manner. When you are ready to get started, here are some of the steps that you will need to take to use the darknet marketplace.

Downloading the Tor Browser

Using either a Mac or Windows operating system can compromise some of the security that comes with using darknet, so it is best if you can use one of the Linux systems like TAILS or Ubuntu. The standard protocol for the Internet is not going to allow you to access the darknet markets. The Tor network is going to require the Tor browser to get ahold of some of this hidden content. The good news is that this browser is available for you to use on any of the operating systems for free. The TAILS, which is the best option to use with this, will come installed with your Tor browser. To get this on your computer, use these steps:

- Choose the operating system currently on your computer and then download the right browser based on the specs of your computer.
- Then you can extract the download with the help of an extracting program like the Archive Manager.
- Extract the files out of the archive.

- Now you can click on the most recent file to open it. The window should come up, and you can click on "run" to get this going.

Browsing Through this Marketplace

There are some different options you can make when it comes to browsing through the marketplace, but we are going to choose Agora to make it easier. To start browsing through the Agora marketplace, use the following steps:

- Load up the main page that comes with Agora, making sure you use your downloaded Tor browser. When you get here, click on register.
- There are some times when these registrations are going to require you to have a special link for a referral. The good news is that you can find these links on the Agora forum if you look under the referral links board.
- You can then enter the details that you would like to use on the following page before clicking on register.
- Now you are ready to log on to the website.

Purchase the Bitcoin

At this point, we have talked about some of the methods that you can choose to purchase the Bitcoin that you would like to use. You can go through and use the exchange that you would like or find someone who is willing to meet with you face to face to sell the Bitcoin that you are going to use.

Many of these marketplaces are going to be easy to use with your Bitcoin wallet so make sure that it is set up for all the purchases.

Step by Step Process

I will use Coinbase for illustration purposes. This is how to use an exchange website to obtain Bitcoin.

To be able to access the buy/sell service you will have to provide the company with your bank data. You will also need photo identification and to set up a two-factor verification on your phone.

Visit the website and set up a new wallet. To do so, insert your name, email address and a strong password. Once you have no issue with the User Agreement, then complete the process.

A link will be sent to your email address. Click the link to confirm that your address is valid. Sign in. At the top on the left-hand side, you will see a tab that says Buy/Sell Bitcoin. Select that tab then select another tab that says Complete now. That button should be able to be found on the right side of the screen.

For every step, provide the necessary details. When your account details have been confirmed after a few days, select the Buy/Sell Bitcoin tab to purchase Bitcoins. The funds will be deposited after several days.

Bitquick is another company that is like Coinbase. They operate in the USA whereas Coinbase is global. Whichever company you prefer, always know what fees are associated with your purchases.

Another Alternative

If you wish to be a bit more private, another service provider is LocalBitcoins. Advertisements are usually placed on the website along with the exchange rate. You can respond to the advertisement and meet the individual to buy Bitcoins with cash. Or you can use online banking to pay for them. There is also a conflict-resolution platform and escrow service. The reason for this alternative option is that you won't have to use your real name and address.

Go to the website localbitcoins.com and set up a new account. Confirm your email address by clicking the link that is sent to you. They have more than 240 countries listed. On the main page, you will provide the amount, the currency, the location, and payment options.

Payment options that are provided include Moneygram, Western Union, cash by mail, cash deposit, PayPal, bank transfers or other online payment. There is the "in person" option as previously mentioned. Select which one applies to you. Select the Find Offers tab on the main page. Once you have chosen a reputable seller, select the Buy tab located on the right-hand side. Review the seller's terms and send a message to complete the process. Monitor your dashboard to be alerted when you have a new message. Then finalize the sale.

Be aware that just like any other service provider, there will be pros and cons. I have already noted that the advantages are that it is private and there are various payment options. The downside is that the fee can be high when purchasing with cash. Moreover, though the company does not ask for your identification, some sellers may do so when a large purchase is made.

Another option is Wall of Coins that is available in 12 countries including the United States and the United Kingdom, Canada, Australia, and Germany. You will need to provide a phone number to buy. You will be asked about your location, and you can simply insert your zip code. The location is requested, to find the banks that are closest to you. The waiting time for delivery of coins is about 15 minutes.

Set Up the PGP Encryption

This step is not required, but it is highly recommended because it is going to help you to keep your address and your identity secure on the marketplace so you should consider using it. The PGP encryption will allow you to send your address and other personal information securely using a system of key encryption. It isn't always something necessary to use with your vendors, many of them will ask you to have it before purchasing one of their products. There is some open source software available for all the major operating systems that will help you to get PGP set up. There is also an applet available for JavaScript that you can use.

When you want to create a two-factor authentication, which is often required to make purchases on this marketplace and for some of the tumbler services that you will use, you need to make sure that you have your own public key and you will need to use the PGP.

How to Transfer the Bitcoin

Before you can make any purchases and get the item that you would like, you need to make sure that you are using the wallet that you created (perhaps through Coinbase or another service). You will need to transfer this wallet over into the wallet of the marketplace. This is possible to do with either the 26 or the 35-character Bitcoin addresses as long as you do it through the send Bitcoins link there. It can sometimes take a few hours for this to get done, though, but it works well.

To make sure that you are keeping this as secure as possible, it is a good idea to use a separate service to tumble the Bitcoins, and Helix is a good one to use. This is a good idea because it helps to make all your personal details are untraceable. This is not a requirement, but it does add an extra level of protection that you are working with. When you are ready to set up the Helix service, follow these steps:

- You will need to visit gramsflow.com inside of your Tor browser to get to the Grams by Helix. This is going to redirect you over to Grams, and you can go to their login page before selecting the right registration link.
- Take the PGP address and copy it. Enter this into the login form and add in the other information that you need here.
- Once this is done, you are going to receive an address that will allow you to send over a small amount of Bitcoin (just a few dollars or less) so that you can confirm that the transaction is secure. Once this is confirmed, you will get the money put back in the account.
- It may take a bit of time before the blockchain can confirm this deposit so don't be impatient.
- Once your deposit has had time to be confirmed into the blockchain, you will need to decrypt a certain PGP message sent to you. You will be able to do this with the

PGP key. Simply copy and then paste the message into the clipboard for the GPA and then select to have it decrypted.

- Once you enter this information, you will be sent over to the main dashboard in Grams. Here you will be able to see the deposit address if you received two confirmations for that original deposits or you will be able to check here until it is all confirmed.

- Now go to the wallet and deposit the amount that you want to keep in there. You can choose any amount to help make things easier, but most will choose to find the product first and place just that amount inside the account to keep it easier. It should only take a few minutes before this transaction shows up on the blockchain.

- As soon as you receive two confirmations, it is going to be possible to withdraw this amount.

- When you are ready to withdraw, you can go to the Helix withdrawal page. Enter the address that you want to send this money to, as well as the amount that you are going to pay them.

- If you are sending this money to a one-use wallet, such as what is found in the Evolution marketplace, you should select that this is a one transaction option. Once you send this out, the Helix program is going to tumble the Bitcoin message so that no one can figure out where the transaction came from.

Making Purchases on the Marketplace

Now that you have deposited some money into the account, it is time to purchase some of the products that you would like to use so that you can send the money over to them and get the product. We are again going to use the Agora marketplace to keep things a bit easier. One note as a beginner, avoid making purchases from vendors who want you to finalize early on. This is an easy way to get scammed because you will go outside of the escrow system and since it is hard to figure out who each person is in the marketplace because of the way Bitcoin and its transactions are set up, you will pretty much just be out of the money without any help.

To get started on the marketplace and to make some purchases, you will need to use the following steps:

- Search for the items that you want. You can use the navigation menu to the left of your screen to find what you would like to use.
- There are some different sorting options that you can go with. You can change the sorting options to be whatever you would like, but make sure that the "No-FE first" box is marked off.
- After you find an item that you like and you click on it,

you should not only check if the item matches your needs, but read some of the feedback and the profile page of the vendor. You don't want to make a purchase from a vendor that has a bad reputation on here.

- While you are there with the vendor's page, copy the PGP address provided because you will need this later. Save that address into a .txt file using either mousepad or notepad so that you can reach it later.

- If you have decided to use this vendor, you can open up the PGP client and then go to the section that says "Keys" before selecting on "Import Keys." You can then import the .txt file that you saved earlier so that you have the PGP key of the vendor.

- Once this is imported, go to the Windows part and then click on Clipboard. Once this is open, click on the File before selecting Encrypt. You are going to encrypt the vendors key at this point.

- Now you can select the product that you would like to purchase by clicking on the "buy" button beneath the listed item. This is going to allow you to see the complete price of the product along with the shipping.

- At this point, you will be able to paste the address that you encrypted into the screen and then press "Preview" to continue. You will be asked to enter your pin number before pressing on "Confirm" to place this order.

At this point, you are all set up to make the purchase that you would want, but now it is time to move on to double checking the order and getting everything finalized so that the payment goes through and you receive your product as soon as possible.

Finalizing the Purchase

You are going to finalize the purchase into the escrow system. This is a great option because it makes sure the vendor is going to get paid for the service or the product they promised, but it also gives you a chance to get the money back if something goes wrong and you don't get the product. Remember that when a transaction is done in Bitcoin, it doesn't have a reverse button to help get the money back. The escrow can help you out if the product doesn't come, if you are dissatisfied, or if something else goes wrong, you can still get the money back during its time in escrow. It shows the buyer that you can pay so that once you get the item, they will receive the money.

Once you get the item, you are going to be responsible for finalizing the whole purchase. To do this, you will need to log back into Agora once you get the product in the mail. From Agora, you can click on the link for orders right at the top of this page. You should be able to see a big list of orders (or just one order if that is all you have done up to this point). Make sure to click on the "Details" button right next to the order over to the right side.

One thing to keep in mind is you can ask the vendor for an extension on the escrow because you haven't received the order, or you are working with Agora in a resolving process. This automatic function is going to happen 13 days after the purchase, and then the money is going to be sent over to the seller. It can be hard to get this back at this point so stay on top of your purchases and make sure that you get them.

Now, if you got the purchase, you can scroll over to the bottom of the order and look for the red button that says Finalize on it. You can click on this to tell the system you received the order, and you are satisfied with it. You can then confirm that the money inside of the escrow can be sent over to the vendor.

Make sure that at this time you rate the vendor and leave your feedback. This only takes a few minutes but can help the other buyers to learn more about the vendor and to figure out if they are the right one to work with. Many people will take the time to leave feedback if they aren't happy with the vendor, but most will ignore it if the seller does a good job. Help them out on the system, as well as the other buyers, but leaving a little review about how the transaction went with this vendor.

And that is all that you will need to do to make purchases on the Darknet marketplace. Remember that we only used the Agora system for this one, but it is going to work about the same with a lot of the other marketplaces that you want to use inside of this system. You can just go through some of the same steps to make these marketplaces work, and since they are similar, you should be just fine. You can continue to go through these steps each time that you want to make a purchase inside of this system.

The Bitcoin system of currency is one of the best ones to use on marketplaces like the darknet marketplace because this currency is going to allow you and the seller to remain completely anonymous and it is hard to trace where the money is going between them. If you are on a market like Darknet, it is a good idea to use all the precautions, and the Tor browser, to make sure that your transactions are safe and secure from others who may want to know what you are up to. Darknet and Bitcoin combined is the perfect solution.

Chapter 6

How to Get Tipped, Earn from Interest Payments, and Trading with Bitcoin

In addition to being able to sell a product or a service to earn Bitcoin, it is also possible to use several other methods to get the Bitcoin that you need to make an income or to make some of the purchases that you need. You can earn Bitcoin when you lend money to someone else and charge interest on it and even when you do some trading. Let's look at how some of these will work if you are considering earning some more Bitcoin.

Trading to Earn Bitcoin

Another option that you can use to earn Bitcoin is trading. Keep in mind that this is almost like a form of gambling, but there are some differences you will encounter. When you are gambling, as long as it is a fair game, you are going to have a set probability of either losing or winning depending on the game that you play. When you are trading your assets, the issue is going to get into more complex issues.

The best and safest way to make some money with trading is through the process of arbitrage. This process is when you see that there is an opportunity to buy a new asset in one place for a low price and then right after you make the purchase, you will sell it in another location where you can make more out of it. It is important that before you do this, you know that you will be able to sell the asset at a higher price right away. If you just make purchases and don't know that you can make a profit out of it, you are basically gambling, and that is not a good way to earn more Bitcoin.

There are many arbitrage situations that you can use. You can be on a few different ties and see that the service or product is for one price in one location, but there are people who would pay more for it if you offered. But it is not as simple as you would think. You need to recognize the value of the products that you are working with and be sure that you are getting one for a great deal and would be able to sell it for more right away in another location. If you have a good mind for business and understanding how this all works, it can be a good option, but you need to be careful.

Simple speculation is also a good trading method that you can use in Bitcoin. With speculation, you will purchase Bitcoins at one price and then hold onto them until the price starts to increase. You can then sell the currency for a higher price and make a profit. You would keep on doing this any time that the price for the Bitcoins go down and then sell them as soon as the price goes up. You need to be good at guessing the Bitcoin market (and remember that it isn't always going to work the same as the market with traditional currencies) so that you can guess what is going to happen in the future with some accuracy. Otherwise, you are just losing money.

If you would like to get started in trading, you need to learn how to read the market of Bitcoin and learn how to recognize the patterns that occur. This is specialized work and only some people who are used to doing research and recognizing trends are going to do well with it. You can make some good money off the process, but you need to be careful that you are taking your time and thinking things through with your trades if you would like to see results with them.

Different Approaches to Trading

Bandwagon

Bandwagon is the term used when traders support whatever is trending. Individuals make choices based on what other people expect from them. So, if most people are engaging in a certain practice, and you follow, then the term applies to your behavior. The term applies even though you have your own personal reservations.

The Herd Mentality

Have you ever seen cattle grazing, one hears a sound and starts running? A few others follow because they do not want to remain behind. Suddenly, all the animals that were once settled in the field are creating a stampede. Likewise, with this type of trading approach, individuals rush and conduct certain practices without a proper plan. Such behavior can cause a market to crash.

Loss Aversion

This is when an individual prefers to cut his profit and stay with the loss. It is also referred to like the prospect theory.

Focusing

At times, you will seek information about something, but there isn't much which you can find. When you do find a little nugget of information, you may tend to hold on to it for dear life. This is so because it is the only available information. Focusing is the trading term.

Idealist

This is when everything you do seems rosy. Life is great, and you have high expectations. They are so high that you are not levelheaded in your thinking and this may cause you not to make proper decisions. Be mindful that there may be negative results so do not focus on the positive only. Practice being objective.

Denial

Do not become so attuned to making money that you bury your head when you should be paying attention. When you see red flags, be alert and research properly.

Over Confidence

On the other end of the spectrum, is being too confident about certain investments. When you are overconfident, you tend to ignore certain signs. Learn from previous mistakes and people's experience. Maintain a balanced approach and look at various angles before deciding.

Using Interest to Earn Bitcoins

If you already own some Bitcoins from another endeavor that you worked on, you may want to put the Bitcoins to work for you. If you are willing to lend out some of these Bitcoins to other people and place an interest amount on it, you will be able to make some money on the money that you let other people borrow from you. Some of the ways that you can make interest money income from Bitcoins include:

Lending it directly

The first way to make this work is to lend the money directly to someone that you already know. You will already be familiar with the person, and you can determine if they are going to be good at returning the money. You both will be able to make up the terms of the agreement, such as the amount of interest they will pay and how long the loan is good for. You may have trouble finding people who would want to borrow the Bitcoins and meet up with your terms, but this is a good place to get started.

Peer to peer lending

The next option is to work on peer to peer lending. There are websites that will have a list of borrowers who are looking for someone to lend to them. Borrowers are going to publish their requests for funding, and you can give some of the money or all of it depending on how much you have available, and they will give you a portion of the interest payments, in addition to the original amount you provided, over the terms of the agreement. You will be able to see the reason for the loan being requested, how long the terms should be good for and the interest rate that the borrower will pay to you and the other lenders.

Borrowers need funding for several reasons including new business venture, trading, building a mining platform, car financing, credit card financing, and medical expenses.

Two platforms for this type of lending are Bitbond and BTCjam. Bitbond is a regulated financial entity that is based in Berlin, Germany and offers as much as 13% interest for lending. The company has over 90, 000 registered users in more than 120 countries. Bitbond terms are in various categories, and they are six weeks, six months, one year, three years, and five years.

There are other platforms which you can research. Always ensure that whichever platform you use, you properly check the reputation and status of the entity. For example, BitLendingClub was a huge platform in Bulgaria that which was launched in 2014. It assisted small businesses to gain access to funding. They rebranded in 2015.

In 2016 the company announced that it would no longer operate because of "regulatory pressures" though no description of what pressure the company encountered was conveyed to the public. A period was given for limited functionality to allow borrowers to repay loans and withdraw funds among other things. You do not want to get entangled with any platform that will have you on edge as to whether they are about to cease operation. You also do not want a situation where you are not given enough time to take certain actions. Choose your platform wisely.

Things to do

These are some pointers for peer to peer lending:

- Always investigate the borrower before investing.
- Be attentive to what the borrower communicates. If something doesn't correlate or the information

sounds strange, do not invest if you're unsure of what is being conveyed.

- Be inquisitive. Do not neglect to ask the right questions so that you can make an informed decision.
- Expand your base. It is more prudent to invest in several small amounts than in an individual with a huge amount.
- Realize that the higher the interest rate, the higher will be the risk
- Don't invest more than you are willing to part with. I addressed the issue of trying to recoup a repayment.
- Do not auto invest unless you are okay with taking such risk.
- Be very cautious about investing in an individual who hasn't repaid a loan in the past. That is a red flag.
- If the borrower does not have a good trust rating, reconsider about investing.

These are some indicators of whether the borrower has a good trust rating:

- Identity is valid. Proof includes a government issued identification.
- Proof that address, income, telephone and email address is valid.

- Authentication of a credit card.
- Social media presence such as Facebook, Twitter, etc.

The advantages of using Bitcoin lending platforms:

- It's easy. There is no charge for the lender. On the other hand, the borrower pays from around 1% - 5%.
- You will receive a higher interest rate. The normal rates are around 3% - 7%. Some platforms offer more.
- It's a faster process than other financial entities.

For illustration purposes, I will use BTCjam. Go to the website and set up an account. Select Invest and then Strat Investing to generate an account. Insert your personal information in the boxes provided. Once you agree to the Terms and Conditions, check the box next to it. Your next step is to click the Sign Up.

BTCjam would send a link to the email address you provided. Confirm your email address by clicking the link. When you've done this, the next process is for you to deposit Bitcoins for the loan.

Familiarizing Yourself with The Dashboard

On the dashboard, on the left side will be your name and below a section that says Reputation. On the right-hand side will be a section that says Account Balance. In the center, you will see a tab that says Deposit Bitcoin. Select the Add Funds tab.

When the pop-up window appears, you will see an address. That's the address where you will send the Bitcoin. After several minutes have passed, your deposit will be made. Then you can invest.

Investing

On the tab where you see the BTCjam logo, there is a button on the right that says Invest. After you select that button, you will see the loan listings. On the left is a box that says filter with various categories. These classifications include the period for the loan, the borrower's rating, the currency value in which the loan should be advanced. The time frame categories for the loan are 1-2 months, 3-4 months, and 6 months - 1 year.

You will see the Bitcoin Loan Listings of borrowers, a section for interest yield and time remaining on the loan. When you have chosen the one you want, select the name.

The next window that will appear is the rating. You can view whether the borrower's income, identity, credit card, social media is verified. Additionally, it shows references and whether the profile is filled out entirely. You can also view the borrower's reputation and the borrower's explanation which is in a box that says Description.

If you are satisfied with the information, select Invest and put the amount you are investing. Select the Invest tab again.

After investing a window appears letting you know that the process has been completed.

Auto Invest

Two tabs will appear Browse Listing and Set Up Auto Invest. You can review other listings if you would like to diversify. Auto invest is an automated investment procedure that is determined by the risk you want to take. Options include conservative, moderate and aggressive. There is a section for you to enter the amount after which you must choose the Activate Plan tab to complete it.

There is a tab that says Payment where you can change the date of payment.

Default

When a borrower doesn't repay, the next step is arbitration. The borrower is sued by the arbitrator in the borrower's location to recover the financing. When the borrower is not from your country, however, it can be very challenging and sometimes futile. Be knowledgeable about who you are too and the implications when the borrower doesn't comply.

Do a Bitcoin bank

With this option, you are going to take the Bitcoins that you would like to deposit in a bank that will pay you an interest rate on the amount that you leave there. This method can ensure that you are going to make the return on investment agreed to at the beginning, but it is often lower than the other options. It is nice because you will be able to trust the bank, the one borrower, and they are often going to be more selective of the people they lend out the money to since they have to pay that interest back, which makes for a more secure investment for you. This is a good way to begin building your currency before using some of the other options to make a better return on investment.

There are advantages and disadvantages to using exchanges. It allows for easy trading of bitcoins and fiat currency. The downside is that there are risks. One threat to this process is the bank run. If everyone wants their money all at once, the bank won't be able to meet that demand. The bank only keeps a fractional reserve. This can create a panic. As a result, individuals may hurriedly withdraw their funds to prevent any losses. This would cause a strain on the bank's level of operation.

Be vigilant of which bank you use. Bank owners can be fraudsters operating a Ponzi scheme. There is also the probability of the system being hacked.

Tipping

To receive Bitcoins through tips, first set up a platform to receive payment. If you have a small business, such as an online shop or a physical shop, follow the following procedures.

Place the Bitcoin logo that says *Bitcoin accepted here*. Or place a sign that says *We Accept Bitcoin* or any similar wording. If you are newly opened, or your Bitcoin customer base is small, still put up the sign. Doing so creates awareness and gives more options to customers who use it.

Print out and display your QR code with your Bitcoin address. Put it close to your cash register for visibility. Customers with the app on their smartphones can insert the purchase value in EUR or USD. The app will give customers the equivalent amount in Bitcoin. Once paid then you can verify the incoming payment.

Based on which wallet you have, there is a button that says *Create Payment Request* to make it easier. You enter the amount that the customer owes after calculating it. Then you click that tab that says *Receive Money*.

If you have an online store, you can use a Bitcoin merchant solution. Examples include Bitcoin Pay, Bitaps, Cashila, and Coinify. There are many others. Chose the one that is best suited for your needs.

If you send invoices in the mail, consider including it as an option just like how it is done for credit card options.

Years ago, there weren't many things which you could buy with Bitcoins. Since then, Bitcoin has become an alternative form of payment, and there are very interesting and common things which you can buy with it. In 2013, a bar in Australia known as Old Fitzroy became the first of its kind in that country by allowing patrons to make payments for beer with Bitcoin. In certain countries such as Hungary and Argentina, you can pay for a taxi using Bitcoin. One of the Burger King franchises in the Netherlands allows that form of payment. This option was offered in 2016 and customers can pay for a Whopper with it.

You can also purchase airline tickets with certain companies. Individuals in New York can use the Jackpocket app to buy lottery tickets. Some international charities now allow donors to make contributions in Bitcoin. Individuals can also purchase cars and yachts with this type of currency. In this modern time, the options are boundless, and people have favorably changed their way of conducting business. Be progressive and make the necessary changes to receive other alternate payment and keep your customers satisfied.

Fraud Prevention

Be aware that swindlers can send fake invoices. Customers who are unaware can make a payment to someone else instead of you. Avoid having customers typing Bitcoin addresses from the stubs. Allow customers to obtain your entire address via your secure website. Print about five characters from your address. This is so the customer can have a paper trail for their records should a query about the payment arise.

Tipping and receiving

You can receive tips from your physical or online store. When someone wants to tip, you will be able to accept it based on the steps previously discussed. You can receive tips online or with your physical shop. Simply have the all the information visible.

Accept tips from assisting individuals with tasks

There are websites which list certain tasks, and you get paid in Bitcoin. One example is Bitfortip where you can help individuals with their queries. You can also be paid for viewing videos and websites on other websites.

Redeem Them Like Coupons

Let's imagine that you have a café. There is sizeable tip box nicely positioned on the counter to receive money. You can also encourage tipping in Bitcoin. You can print paper vouchers from websites that offer this voucher type of service. The voucher should display certain information such as the balance, and it can be used as a coupon.

These are just a few of the methods that you can use to start earning some Bitcoins. These can be a lot of fun and help you earn a great return on your investment if you pick the right options and make sure that you know the market. You don't want to end up wasting your money on a bad borrower or on purchasing a product you aren't able to sell right away.

Other Books by Author

Go to http://bit.ly/evanlane to check out Evan Lane's Author Central Page, along with his other books

Wireless Hacking: How to Hack Wireless Networks

Python Programming: A Stepy by Step Guide for Beginner's

Hacking with Python: Your Guide to Ethical Hacking, Basic Security, and Python Hacking